Messages for a Happier Life

Inspiring Essays from the Church News by William B. Smart

Deseret Book Company
Salt Lake City, Utah

No part of this book may be reproduced in any
form or by any means without permission in writing
from the publisher, Deseret Book Company,
P.O. Box 30178, Salt Lake City, Utah 84130.
Deseret Book is a registered trademark of
Deseret Book Company.

First printing February 1989

Library of Congress Cataloging-in-Publication Data

Smart, William B. (William Buckwalter), 1922-
    Messages for a happier life.

    Includes index.
    1. Spiritual life—Mormon authors. I. Title.
BX8656.S63 1989   248.4′89332   88-33584
ISBN 0-87579-181-6

CONTENTS

MESSAGES FOR A HAPPIER LIFE

MESSAGES FOR THE FAMILY

MESSAGES FROM OUR HERITAGE

MESSAGES OF LOVE

PREFACE

Happiness, said Joseph Smith, is the object and design of our existence. Lehi said it even more succinctly: Men are that they might have joy.

So here is the universal and unending quest. It's what life is all about.

But people pursue the quest in such different ways. In a Las Vegas casino, vacant-eyed men and women spend hours pulling the handles of slot machines. Half a world away in an Indian hospital, a young volunteer holds in her arms and murmurs loving words to a dying old man. Each is seeking happiness.

Some seek happiness in drugs or liquor, others in tuning the body and spirit for the highest enjoyment of this wondrous world. Some relentlessly pursue wealth and the big boys' toys that go with it; others devote their lives to family and service. Some struggle in hopes of achieving happiness at some future time; others are wise enough to know that the only time happiness can be grasped is here and now.

So the search goes on. In this volume is distilled much of what I have learned in my own personal search.

In briefest summary, it is this: Happiness has little to do with externalities; it is a state of mind. It depends not on what happens to us, but on how we react to what happens. It depends on the clearness of our conscience. And the primary truth: We are happy to the extent we get beyond and above ourselves by reaching out to others and up to God.

That is what I have tried to say, in many different ways, in this collection of short essays, almost all of which were first published as the back-page "Viewpoint" of the Church News. I am indebted to officers of the Deseret News—President Thomas S. Monson, Elder James. E. Faust, and Publisher William James Mortimer—and to Church News Editor Dell Van Orden for the privilege of contributing to this column, for encouragement to publish this book, and for helpful critique and counsel.

I am indebted to family, friends, and loved associates for ideas contributed and for being living examples of the values reflected here.

And, most of all, I am forever indebted to my best earthly friend and source of inspiration, my wife, Donna.

MESSAGES
OF HOPE

FOR THY SAKE

Look," came the voice from the back row of the high priests group meeting. "If you or I saw someone suffering and didn't help, we'd be under condemnation, right? Well, when God could help, why doesn't He?"

A provocative question, one that has troubled man for centuries.

Why does the Lord allow such awesome tragedies as the volcano eruption in Colombia? The genocides in Eastern Europe, Cambodia, Uganda? The famines in Africa? Why do innocent people die in terrorist attacks? Why are good people killed or maimed in auto accidents, or ravaged by agonizing terminal illnesses, or tormented by the tearing apart of marriages and homes?

The answer is, we don't know. It is not given to man to know the mind of God, and agonizing over the meaning or cause of this disaster or that suffering can be fruitless and destructive.

But some reflection on the nature of adversity may be helpful. There is a law irrevocably decreed in heaven, Section 130 of the Doctrine and Covenants tells us. We must suppose the Lord is bound by that law, just as He told us, "I, the Lord, am bound when ye do what I say." Part of that law, it would seem, is that growth and strength can come only by overcoming resistance. Just as the muscles of the arm can become strong

3

only by exercising against resistance, so is striving against adversity essential to the growth of man. As one author put it, if life were not sometimes hard, we should have no muscles, mental or moral. There is no other way.

The words were carefully chosen when the Lord, in closing the gates of Eden, told us, "cursed be the ground *for thy sake.*" Thorns and thistles followed. So did cruelty and hunger, broken health, lost jobs, thwarted dreams — all, in the long view, for our sake.

Remembering that, it may be easier to keep adversity from becoming tragedy. The difference is fundamental. Adversity is what happens to us. Tragedy is what we allow it to do to us. How we react to adversity determines whether we grow or, by degrees, die.

Example: A thirty-four-year-old man arrested illegally; thrown without trial into a stinking dungeon without windows, heat, or sanitary facilities; a rough stone floor for a bed; food rotting, perhaps poisoned. That's adversity. Out of it came a cry for succor, not despairing but faithful, as poignant as any in religious literature. And out of it came one of the most glorious, comforting, inspiring revelations known to man, one that concludes with these words:

"Let thy bowels also be full of charity towards all men . . . let virtue garnish thy thoughts unceasingly; then shall thy confidence wax strong in the presence of God. . . . The Holy Ghost shall be thy constant companion, and thy scepter an unchanging scepter of righteousness and truth; and thy dominion shall be an everlasting dominion, and without compulsory means it shall flow unto thee forever and ever." (D&C 121:45-46.)

Thus did the Lord acknowledge Joseph Smith's refusal to crumble; thus did triumph arise from adversity.

Adversity will come; it is part of the divine scheme of things. The challenge is to make of it triumph, not tragedy.

ANTIDOTES TO ADVERSITY

Adversity is part of life. It comes at different times, in different forms, in varying degrees of intensity. But come it does, to all of us.

The great challenge is to refuse to let the bad things that *happen* to us do bad things *to* us. That is the crucial difference between adversity and tragedy.

How can we preserve the difference?

In one of those senior citizen magazines, picked up in a doctor's waiting room, was an article on how to grow old gracefully. The prescription could be summarized in three words: fitness, friends, purpose. The same elements are vital in coping with adversity.

Adversity becomes tragedy if it destroys mental or emotional health. Mental health depends, to a considerable extent, on physical health. Good diet, regular exercise, adequate sleep—these are essentials of good health that are too often neglected under the stress of adversity. But fitness is more important at those times than at any other.

So are friends. The man or woman invites tragedy who, at times of illness, death, lost jobs, broken homes, withdraws into self. The brotherhood and sisterhood of the gospel is never more priceless than at such times when it is needed most. Social aloneness leads to aloneness of the spirit, and that is the ultimate tragedy.

Purpose is the enemy of despair. The man who lives mostly for and in himself is left desolate when that pertaining to himself—his health, his income, his reputation or power—is attacked or lost. But if his motivation is higher and broader, there is still purpose after these are gone. And purpose is the fuel without which progress stops and decay begins.

So fitness, friends, purpose; to these add perspective. Trouble that seems overwhelming, grief that seems unbearable, somehow becomes more manageable when seen in the majestic context of the Lord's creation. One troubled soul may find that perspective in the view from a hard-won mountain peak. Another from a worshipful walk under a starry sky. Or from pondering the wonder of a rosebud. Or standing in awe of a newborn baby. Or being soul-washed by the gift of music or art that speaks so eloquently of the genius with which God has entrusted man.

A thing of beauty, wrote John Keats in "Endymion: A Poetic Romance," is a joy forever. It is even more than a joy. The beauty, the balance, the wonder of what the Lord has created can be a healing balm. As Keats wrote:

> Therefore, on every morrow, are we wreathing
> A flowery band to bind us to the earth,
> Spite of despondence, of the inhuman dearth
> Of noble natures, of the gloomy days,
> Of all the unhealthy and o'er-darken'd ways
> Made for our searching: yes, in spite of all,
> Some shape of beauty moves away the pall
> From our dark spirits . . .

Finally, adversity becomes tragedy in its most virulent form when it destroys self-image, when it makes us doubt our worth, doubt we are loved by God or by family or friends. Then, when the paralyzing conviction grows that no one cares, the Destroyer has his greatest opportunity.

When grief and despair make the heavens seem closed,

the struggle to open them is hardest — and most essential. Then is when the scriptures and prayer have their greatest saving power. Then is when the soul most needs to open to the assuring whisper, "I am a child of God."

SEEING AS THE LORD SEES

Until that night, Don had it all.

Handsome, gregarious, athletically and mentally gifted, well launched in a prosperous career, blessed with a lovely wife and family, he was, in his early thirties, on his way.

Then came the night. Don went to bed. He awoke the next morning, blind. A rare disease had destroyed his optic nerve.

Some men would have been destroyed. Not Don. He went back to school, earned a law degree, launched a new career. For him, the principle of compensation held true—that when one sense is lost, the others are sharpened. With sight gone, hearing and touch and smell grew amazingly acute.

For years, until other physical problems stopped him, he skied Utah mountains, following the tinkling of bells attached to his partner's boots. Still today, he shoots golf in the low 80s, hitting in the direction his partner points, feeling the contour of the green through the soles of his feet, putting to the sound of a club rattled in the cup.

In a way sighted people can never understand, the loss of his physical eyes sharpened the vision of his inner eye. He "sees" the golf course, the shot he is about to hit, the problems in daily living and human relations more clearly and accurately than the rest of us.

Without many of the distractions others experience, he can see things as they really are. That focus seems to give him a special keenness of discernment and empathy that attract people to him for counsel and encouragement.

Was it not something like this that the Apostle Paul meant when he wrote: " . . . We look not at the things which are seen, but at the things which are not seen: for the things which are seen are temporal [and, being temporal, subject to error and misinterpretation]; but the things which are not seen are eternal." (2 Cor. 4:18.)

Paul had reason to know the difference. After years of seeing things wrong, and doing terrible wrongs as a result, he, too, was suddenly stricken blind. In the moment of his sight loss and in the three days that followed, he began to see as he had never seen before.

It took fervent prayer during those three days of darkness for spiritual sight to develop. And then it took something more: "And Ananias went his way, and entered into the house; and putting his hands on him said, Brother Saul, the Lord, even Jesus, that appeared unto thee in the way as thou camest, hath sent me, that thou mightest receive thy sight, and be filled with the Holy Ghost.

"And immediately there fell from his eyes as it had been scales: and he received sight forthwith, and arose, and was baptized." (Acts 9:17-18.)

The connection is clear: Full spiritual sight follows faith, prayer, baptism and the gift of the Holy Ghost. Armed with such sight, Paul began one of the greatest missionary careers in recorded scripture.

So what is our task, those of us blessed with all our physical senses? Surely, it is to use what we have been given. May we not be among those of whom the Lord said: "Eyes have they, but they see not: They have ears, but they hear not: noses have they, but they smell not." (Ps. 115:5-6.)

Beyond that, may we, like Don, develop the inner eye to see things as they really are. And ultimately, as we struggle toward perfection, may we strive to see as the Lord sees, "for

9

man looketh on the outer appearance, but the Lord looketh on the heart." (1 Sam. 16:7.)

Then may we reach the highest good to which Paul, with his spiritually enlarged vision, aspired—to truly know God, and our fellowmen, and ourselves. "For now we see through a glass, darkly; but then face to face: now I know in part; but then shall I know even as also I am known." (1 Cor. 13:12.)

ARE WE NOT ALL BEGGARS?

She's a woman who, one would think, has it all. She has health, beauty, wealth, talent. Her home is impeccable; her husband loving, decent, faithful; her children capable; her grandchildren adoring and adorable. She is loved and admired by all who know her. Who could ask for more?

To a close—and very surprised—friend, she confided: "I struggle so with depression. Some days I feel like I can't bear to leave the house. I want to climb in bed and pull the covers over my head."

Depression. It's a burden carried by so many. Often there's no outward sign, and the burden is carried alone, with few to know or understand or help.

Someone sprains an ankle and shows up with a limp and a cane. There's sympathy and understanding and patience with his slower pace. There's great care not to jostle him, especially not to further bruise the injured part.

But all of us have injured parts. We carry within us bruised psyches, hidden insecurities, feelings more tender and vulnerable—and sometimes more painful—than any taped ankle. The man hurrying grimly along the street may need far more understanding and patience than the one limping along with his cane.

True depression is an extreme form of inner bruise, full of pain, slow and difficult to heal. Its causes may be complex—

11

chemical imbalance, for example—and may respond only to professional care. The sufferer is often powerless to help himself. Friends and loved ones can only respond with the kind of loving care that any ill person deserves.

For others, a deeper understanding of who and what we are may help. We may need a clearer realization of our nothingness.

What kind of statement is that? some will ask. One of the deepest symptoms, if not causes, of depression is a conviction of worthlessness. How can more of the same help?

Consider this: The person who relies on his own strength, his own intelligence, his own goodness or importance, is vulnerable. As any part of that strength or intelligence or goodness or importance is stripped away—as it inevitably is—he becomes diminished. He can become, in his own eyes, worthless. Severe emotional problems can follow.

God has provided a better way. King Benjamin spoke of it in his address to the Nephites: " . . . as ye have come to the knowledge of the glory of God, or if ye have known of his goodness and have tasted of his love, and have received a remission of your sins, which causeth such exceedingly great joy in your souls, even so I would that ye should remember, and always retain in remembrance, the greatness of God, and your own nothingness, and his goodness and long-suffering towards you, unworthy creatures, and humble yourselves even in the depths of humility, calling on the name of the Lord daily . . . if ye do this ye shall always rejoice, and be filled with the love of God. . . . " (Mosiah 4:11-12.)

The message is that we are nothing without God, but that with Him and through Him we are everything, made in His image, worthy of His whole redeeming mission and sacrifice. With the humility of that perspective, we can find peace. We can live with our weaknesses because we lean on so much more than our own strength.

He invites us to make Him our foundation, and that foundation cannot be shaken. We cannot be stripped of self-image

12

when we know that all upon which our self-image is based is gifted from God. "For behold, are we not all beggars? Do we not all depend upon the same Being, even God . . . for all the riches we have of every kind?" (Mosiah 4:19.)

DESPERATION IS FOR UNBELIEVERS

Cutting across the mountainous border separating Pakistan and Afghanistan lies the Khyber Pass, the historic invasion route from Central Asia into India. Alexander the Great crossed that pass. So did the Huns, then Tamerlane, then the Mogul emperors who stamped Islam onto much of India and most of what is now Pakistan.

In recent years, a different kind of fighting raged along those passes as Afghanistan tribesmen battled to throw off a foreign yoke from their country. Their courage and determination prevailed; the invaders finally left in defeat.

But the war left a bitter legacy. Sprawling below the Khyber Pass, the fabled city of Peshawar is still crowded with refugees. The victims are easy to spot—men clumping around on one leg, children missing hands—maimed by mines sown by enemy planes. On a dusty Peshawar street, the Afghan Surgical Hospital houses the most severely injured. Some without eyes, some with faces burned away, some with brain damage or internal injuries, many with missing limbs, they lie in crowded wards, stolidly waiting for healing through surgical and medical skills, time, and faith.

Especially faith. That's the one common denominator that permeates every ward of this grim place. Twice a day, everything stops. The staff and all patients who are able move to

14

the courtyards, kneel with foreheads to the ground, facing Mecca. Those who can't assemble turn in their beds.

These were warriors in what their Muslim leaders called a *jihad*, a holy war. They are men qualified in the crucible of pain to testify to the message of the Arabic banner hanging above the courtyard:

> Desperation is only for unbelievers
> Those who believe in God never lose heart

Fanaticism can, and often does, grow from such faith. The world has seen, and deplores, the atrocities fanaticism spawns. That's the dark side. But no one can witness the struggle these fighters waged against such desperate odds, in hospital wards as well as the battlefield, without getting the all-important message that cuts across all religious, racial, and national lines: *Courage comes from faith.*

That's how it is with believers. But we profess to be believers, too. Is our faith as strong as theirs? Avoiding fanaticism, does it make our lives as courageous?

We fight no holy wars of knife and gun to test our courage. But tests come to everyone, in many ways. We see them every day, in our own lives and the lives of those around us.

There's the family whose strong, loving, nurturing father is taken by death. The calm strength, the bonding, the mutual support that turn tragedy into a blessing come from courage born of faith.

There's the neighbor whose heart was dying within her and who, while awaiting the miracle of a suitable donor for a transplant, blessed all around her with her radiant optimism.

There's the other neighbor left desolate when her husband rejected and left her after thirty years of marriage, who emerged from the crucible strengthened spiritually and in every other way.

There's the mother driven frantic by a teenage daughter hooked on drugs and who knows what else, whose neighbors rallied around in regular sessions of fasting and prayer, and who, while the battle isn't over, appears to be winning.

These, too, are believers. Not for them desperation. Faith gives them courage. Courage makes them strong.

That's what the Lord wants and expects. When Joshua faced his greatest test, leading Israel across the Jordan against over-whelming odds, he heard four times in one brief passage the message: Be strong and courageous.

To believers everywhere as they face their trials rings the same assurance He gave to Joshua: "Have not I commanded thee? Be strong and of a good courage; be not afraid, neither be thou dismayed: for the Lord thy God is with thee whith-ersoever thou goest." (Josh. 1:9.)

GOSPEL
MESSAGES

ARE WE, TOO, ASLEEP?

How could they have slept, that night in Gethsemane? These three, Peter, James, and John, were His closest disciples, the three chosen to lead the continuation of His work. They had climbed the mountain with Him, had witnessed there the glory of His Transfiguration, had heard the voice of the Father testifying to His divine Sonship. "But Peter and they that were with him were heavy with sleep." (Luke 9:32.)

Now, in the garden, the most sacred event in all human history was unfolding. In unimaginable agony, Jesus set about the task He had come to earth to do. His soul sorrowful unto death, pressed to the utmost limit of His endurance, Jesus faced His greatest trial, alone. Three times Jesus returned from the awesome struggle to find the disciples asleep.

Why? How could they?

In this luminous sentence from his great work, *The Life and Times of Jesus The Messiah*, Alfred Edersheim suggests an answer: "While He lay in prayer, they lay in sleep; and yet where soul-agony leads not to the one, it often induces the other."

We see so much of that among us: Good people faced with crises that demand earnest, prayerful effort run away instead. In a sense, they sleep, they escape—and become less good as a result.

To truly worship the Savior, to really remember Him, to ponder our debt in appropriate gratitude, is all-important.

So often, however, instead of being led to prayer, we escape into other realms of thought. Often, even in our sacrament meetings, we escape into forms of disturbance that not only kill our own spiritual communion but endanger that of others as well.

We come to His holy house by invitation, to worship, to give thanks, to pledge anew, to show our gratitude by our lives. Our chapels were dedicated, as was the Lord's temple at Kirtland, "that all people who shall enter upon the threshold of the Lord's house may feel thy power, and feel constrained to acknowledge that thou hast sanctified it, and that it is thy house, a place of thy holiness.

"And do thou grant, Holy Father, that all those who shall worship in this house may be taught words of wisdom out of the best books, and that they may seek learning even by study, and also by faith, as thou hast said . . .

"And that this house may be a house of prayer, a house of fasting, a house of faith, a house of glory and of God, even thy house." (D&C 109:13-14, 16.)

Noble purposes, these. They should be, certainly, not too challenging for a people who count themselves among His own. But we are a social people. Visiting comes naturally. Silence is hard, the silence of worship harder still. Sleep is only one of several easy escapes.

How can we consistently take the harder course?

We can't replace something with nothing. It's not enough to empty the mind of the trivialities or worldly concerns that lead us away from worship. We can only stay in tune by filling our minds positively with our awesome debt of gratitude.

We can think of the nails piercing His hands and feet, the spear in His side. We can ponder His love for us, His washing of the feet, His final great prayer interceding with the Father for us. We can rejoice in the glory of the Resurrection.

20

Still, for most of us, sleep will creep up, worldly thoughts will intrude, neighbors will distract.

Then may we invoke the image of our Lord prostrate in the garden, facing, alone, the full power of Satan. Picture it: There lay the Savior in prayer, the disciples in sleep.

For us, which will it be?

TRANSFIGURATION TODAY

After six days Jesus taketh Peter, James, and John his brother, and bringeth them up into an high mountain apart, and was transfigured before them: and his face did shine as the sun, and his raiment was white as the light. (Matt. 17:1-2.)

Those few simple words and the few that follow, telling of the ministering of angels and of the Father's testifying of His Son, are all we know of one of the supreme moments of the Savior's earthly ministry. In some holy, mysterious way, He who was already deeply immersed in His Messiahship received an even higher endowment. Of its meaning we can only stand in wonder and awe.

But in our continuing struggle to follow Him, each of us can, in a sense, experience transfiguration, both of the Savior and of ourselves.

In his superb little book, *The Son of Man*, François Mauriac points out how differently Christ appeared to different people. To a blessed few He appeared as the glorious Messiah; to many as a vagrant and trouble-making Nazarene. To the Samaritan woman at the well, He seemed, at first, an ordinary Jew. When Judas conspired to deliver Him to His enemies, he did not describe His stature or His striking appearance; only by a traitor's kiss could the soldiers distinguish the Son of Man from the eleven poor Jews around Him.

Yet, others loved Him at first sight. Many followed as soon as He began to speak, needing no miracle to prove His divinity. To some, one call only was needed to abandon all they possessed and follow Him.

"He cured many more men born blind than the Gospel recounts," Mauriac wrote. "Each time a creature called Him his Lord and his God and confessed that He was the Christ, the Messiah come into this world, he did so because Christ had opened the interior eye whose vision is not limited simply to appearances."

Whenever came that whispering of the Holy Spirit, whenever scales dropped from the eyes of men and women who then knelt at His feet and accepted Him as their Savior, there was a transfiguration of Jesus.

The same transfiguration blesses believing men and women today. But with the transfiguration, in our hearts, of Jesus, must come a transfiguration of ourselves. The one cannot be fully efficacious without the other.

Alma speaks of this second, personal transfiguration. "Have ye spiritually been born of God?" he challenged his brethren of the Church. "Have ye received his image in your countenances? Have ye experienced this mighty change in your hearts?"

And then, to be certain his listeners understood that this transfiguration must not be a transitory thing, he drove home the point: "If ye have experienced a change of heart, and if ye have felt to sing the song of redeeming love, I would ask, can ye feel so now?" (Alma 5:14, 26.)

The transformation of countenance of those who have experienced this mighty change of heart is remarkable, sometimes almost startling. Who has not seen in a crowded airport or some other place a stranger who was instantly recognized as a fellow Church member? Who has not seen the special glow of peace and calm strength come over the countenance

of one whose life is in harmony with a testimony of the Savior —
or, sadly, the distressing change of countenance of one who,
having had such harmony, has lost it?

With such harmony comes the great blessing of confidence.
It brings confidence in self as a beloved child of God. It brings
confidence in others and our relationships with them, for they,
too, are children of God, our brothers and sisters.

It brings the ultimate confidence, confidence in one's relationship with God. He has clearly told us how to achieve it:
"Let thy bowels also be full of charity towards all men, and to
the household of faith, and let virtue garnish thy thoughts
unceasingly; then shall thy confidence wax strong in the presence of God. . . . " (D&C 121:45.)

Those whose countenances radiate such confidence are
transfigured indeed.

IF ONLY WE HAD BEEN THERE

Tradition has it that when the barbarian Clovis learned, centuries later, of the arrest, trial, and crucifixion of Christ, he clenched his fist and cried: "If only I had been there with my Franks!"

If only he had been there. If only we had been there. Would it have been different?

Had we been at Gethsemane on that moonlit night when Jesus waged His decisive battle with the powers of Satan, what would we have done? When the eternal fate of mankind hung in the balance, when His agony in shouldering our sins was so great He sweat drops of blood, would we have slept?

When He was betrayed by a kiss, bound, and led away, would we have forsaken Him and fled? Fearful of our safety in being associated with such a man, would we have denied knowing Him? How would we have acted had we been there? More to the point, how do we act here and now? The awesome truth is that Gethsemane was not just back then. It is also now. The final act of our redemption is yet to come.

Jesus did His part at Gethsemane. With infinite love and mercy, and infinite pain, He paid His part of the price of our redemption.

There remains our part, including faith, repentance, and righteous works. Unless we pay it, even His supreme sacrifice is powerless to bring us to exaltation.

25

So how faithfully are we paying the price?

"Watch and pray," Jesus enjoined His three chief apostles, "that ye enter not into temptation." (Matt. 26:41.) But they did not. Three times He returned from His divine agony to find them asleep, even as they had slept through that other glorious moment of His ministry on the Mount of Transfiguration.

Watch and pray, He has also enjoined us, for the same reason. Do we? Or do we sleep?

"Let your light so shine before men," He pleaded on another occasion, "that they may see your good works, and glorify your Father which is in heaven." (Matt. 5:16.) Do we? Or when things get sticky, as on that night in Gethsemane, do we silently steal away?

As Paul reminded us, the Lord commanded us to preach to the people, and to testify. (Acts 10:42.) Do we? Or, to save ourselves embarrassment or inconvenience, do we, by our silence, deny we know Him?

Judgment should not be too harsh on those early apostles who slept and fled and denied on that fateful night. They were but human. True, they had sat at His feet and felt His love, had witnessed His miracles. They had heard His own testimony that He was the Son of the Living God, that He had come to save the world. But those are such large truths, so incomprehensibly far beyond their experience.

They could believe these things intellectually, because One whom they loved had told them. But to know them internally, with a certainty that banishes all sleepiness and timidity, perhaps that is too much to expect of unaided mortals.

The aid came, on the day of Pentecost, with the bestowal of the Holy Ghost. With that gift adding spiritual certainty to intellectual assent, the apostles slept or fled or denied no more. Fearless in the armor of God, they and countless followers set about building the kingdom, in total disregard for their own lives.

If only we had been there. But we *are* there. We are there, armed with the same gift of the Holy Ghost that turned fearful disciples into spiritual giants. What will we do about it?

26

LET GO AND REACH UP

It was a family outing in the magnificent red-rock and blue-water country of Utah's Lake Powell, one of many this close-knit family had enjoyed. In one of the lake's lovely coves, the lure of the deep, blue water was strong. The motor was switched off, the houseboat drifted, and everyone went overboard for a swim.

"Everyone" included the family's eighty-five-year-old patriarch. Not much of a swimmer but never one to be left out, he donned a bulbous orange lifejacket and slipped over the side.

The boat's boarding ladder had been lost—no problem for strong young arms and supple bodies when it came time to get back aboard. But for an eighty-five-year-old it was a serious problem.

Grasping a stanchion, the patriarch struggled to climb aboard. Grown sons tried to push from below. Others tried to pull from above, but his white-knuckled grip on the stanchion prevented effective help.

Finally, when his struggles had reached the point of despairing exhaustion, the plea of a daughter came clear: "Dad! Dad! Reach up! Let go and reach up!"

It took faith, in his exhausted condition, to let go of that stanchion, but he did, and reached up. Strong hands grasped his wrists and lifted him into the boat.

27

"Thanks," he gasped as he sprawled on the deck. "I don't know how much longer I could have lasted."

And then, after a long, reflective pause, he seized the teaching moment: "You know, I wonder how many times in my life I have struggled and relied on my own powers when what I needed to do was let go and reach up for help from above."

Through the centuries, men of greatness have been those with the faith to let go and reach up. Abraham, struggling with the awful command to sacrifice his special son, let go and reached up—and heard the ultimate affirmation of his faith: "In thy seed shall all the nations of the earth be blessed; because thou hast obeyed my voice."

Moses, struggling with a stubborn, rebellious people on one hand and an angry and vindictive pharaoh on the other, let go and reached up—and the children of Israel passed through the Red Sea in safety.

The three Hebrews in Nebuchadnezzar's fiery furnace, Daniel in the lion's den, like all the prophets who struggled to bring the Lord's words to an uncaring world, when the crisis came found they had to let go and reach up.

Even the Son of God, our Lord and Savior, after the despairing cry, "My God, why hast thou forsaken me," showed us the way by letting go and reaching up.

And in our time, a fourteen-year-old boy who let go his struggles over the confusion of churches and reached up for help opened the glorious Dispensation of the Fulness of Times.

Do we have the faith to follow these examples as we struggle with our problems? Or are we more like the man who missed his footing at the top of a precipice, plunged over, and saved himself only by clinging to a bush growing out of the cliff?

Feeling the bush slowly give way, he prayed fervently for help and cried, "Isn't there anyone up there who can save me?"

From above came a voice: "I have heard your prayers, my son. Let go of the bush and you will be saved."

A long pause, and then the reply: "Is there anyone else up there?"

"Prove me now herewith," the Lord said, "if I will not open you the windows of heaven and pour you out a blessing, that there shall not be room enough to receive it." (Mal. 3:10.)

And what are the blessings? They are almost beyond counting. The Lord has promised great blessings to those who pay an honest tithe. He has also promised peace to those who follow Him. The Word of Wisdom promises yet other blessings: ". . . they shall find wisdom and great treasures of knowledge, and shall run and not be weary and walk and not faint. . . ."

These and so many other blessings to help through the trials of this life are promised to those with the faith to let go and reach up. Finally, of course, is offered the greatest of all blessings — that whosoever believeth in Him should not perish, but have everlasting life.

OUR GIFTS FROM CHRISTMAS

What did you get for Christmas?

Immediately following the Christmas season you hear this question everywhere as the Western world sets about tidying up after its annual splurge. The more thoughtful among us might ask the question in an importantly different form: What did you get *from* Christmas?

Poor is the man with no one to love him and bring gifts at Christmastime. But poorer still is he who takes from the Christmas experience no lasting values to ennoble his life.

So let's prepare to ask ourselves, when the great day is over, what did we get from Christmas?

Will it be fresh appreciation for the goodness and open-heartedness of people, an appreciation that will make it easier to live in love and harmony with our fellowman as the Savior taught?

Will it be a keener awareness of the want and sadness and loneliness that afflict so many lives—and a greater personal commitment to help? Instead of spending Christmas Eve in the peace and security of their family circle, some will go as volunteers to the rescue mission and other such places where they will serve dinner to homeless, despairing people who will know little peace and security. What they will get from Christmas is the inner glow that comes from emptying our hearts of acquisitiveness and self-centeredness to make room for love and generosity.

At Christmas men come closer than at any other time to the goodwill that God pleads with us to practice at all times. If we get this gift from Christmas, can we keep it glowing throughout the year? Will our gift be new dedication to the great mission that began with His birth: to teach His Gospel and build His kingdom so that through Him all nations of the earth might be blessed? For members of His Church, failure to receive and keep this gift invites condemnation.

Will we get from Christmas a new sense of optimism? Optimism is so much needed today in a world tormented by terrorism, fear of nuclear destruction, drugs, moral breakdown, family disintegration. But the Christmas story reminds us that the world the shepherds knew was pretty dreadful, too, gripped as it was by a tyrant so filled with paranoia and blood-lust that he would shortly order the slaughter of all male infants. To them, in their extremity, came the same message that comes to us in our difficulty: "Fear not: For behold I bring you good tidings of great joy, which shall be to all people." With that divine assurance, who can despair about mankind's future?

The shepherds got something else from Christmas that we, too, can get. They returned to their fields after that visit to the stable, the scriptures tell us, glorifying and praising God.

That was after Christmas was over. But what a glorious gift to take from Christmas and to try to keep throughout the year — a sense of God's power and goodness and mercy, an appreciation of the goodness of His creation, a dedication to do His work, a gratitude so profound that we will return to our fields glorifying and praising God.

Glorifying God is, of course, more than singing praises to His name — though more of that would be good for all of us. It is living so that men might see our good works and glorify our Father which is in heaven. It is filling our souls with the love that leads to godly action. It is doing what we can do to

31

aid in His supreme mission — His glory — to bring to pass the immortality and eternal life of man.

"Glory to God in the highest," peals that glorious Christmas anthem. And what follows? "Peace on earth, good will toward men."

That's what we can get from Christmas.

THREE LEVELS OF CHRISTMAS

Christmas is a beautiful time of the year. We love the excitement, the giving spirit, the special awareness of and appreciation for family and friends, the feelings of love and brotherhood that bless our gatherings at Christmastime.

In all of the joyousness, it is well to reflect that Christmas comes at three levels.

Let's call the first the Santa Claus level. It's the level of Christmas trees and holly, of whispered secrets and colorful packages, of candlelight and rich food and warm open houses. It's carolers in the shopping malls, excited children, and weary but loving parents. It's a lovely time of special warmth and caring and giving. It's the level at which we eat too much and spend too much and do too much—and enjoy every minute of it. We love the Santa Claus level of Christmas.

But there's a higher, more beautiful level. Let's call it the Silent Night level. It's the level of all our glorious Christmas carols, of that beloved, familiar story: "Now in those days there went out a decree from Caesar Augustus. . . . " It's the level of the crowded inn and the silent, holy moment in a dark stable when the Son of Man came to earth. It's shepherds on steep, bare hills near Bethlehem, angels with their glad tidings, a new star in the East, wise men traveling far in search of the Holy One. How beautiful and meaningful it is; how infinitely poorer we would be without this sacred second level of Christmas.

33

The trouble is, these two levels don't last. They can't.

Twelve days of Christmas, at the first level, is about all most of us can stand. It's too intense, too extravagant. The tree dries out and the needles fall. The candles burn down. The beautiful wrappings go out with the trash, the carolers are up on the ski slopes, the toys break, and the biggest day in the stores in the entire year is exchange day, December 26. The feast is over and the dieting begins. But the lonely and the hungry are with us still, perhaps lonelier and hungrier than before.

Lovely and joyous as the first level of Christmas is, there will come a day, very soon, when Mother will put away the decorations and vacuum the living room and think, "Thank goodness that's over for another year."

Even the second level, the level of the Baby Jesus, can't last. How many times this season can you sing "Silent Night"? The angels and the star and the shepherd, even the silent, sacred mystery of that holy night itself, can't long satisfy humanity's basic need. The man who keeps Christ in the manger will, in the end, be disappointed and empty.

No, for Christmas to last all year long, for it to grow in beauty and meaning and purpose, for it to have the power to change lives, we must celebrate it at the third level, that of the *adult* Christ. It is at this level—not as an infant—that our Savior brings His gifts of lasting joy, lasting peace, lasting hope. It was the adult Christ who reached out and touched the untouchable, who loved the unlovable, who so loved us all that even in His agony on the cross He prayed forgiveness for His enemies.

This is the Christ, creator of worlds without number, who wept, Enoch tells us, because so many of us lack affection and hate each other—and then who willingly gave His life for *all* of us, including those for whom He wept. This is the Christ, the adult Christ, who gave us the perfect example, and asked us to follow Him.

Accepting that invitation is the way—the only way—to celebrate Christmas all year and all life long.

34

CHRISTMAS IS HOPE

W hy can't I have everything I want?" the petulant child demanded of the department store Santa Claus.

"Because," came the answer as reported in *USA Today*, "then there would be nothing left to hope for."

Simple as it seems, there may be no more profound way to express the ultimate Christmas message. At both the material and spiritual levels, hope is the essence of Christmas.

Hope is what makes each brightly wrapped package so full of possibilities. For the receiver, anticipation is the magic of Christmas. It is so for the giver as well. The more love and care that have gone into selecting the gift, the keener the anticipation, the hope, that this gift will prove to be exactly right.

In part because of those hopes, Christmas Eve is, in most homes, the best part of Christmas. But there is more, far more.

In the quiet expectancy of Christmas Eve, before the hectic materialism of the day itself, there is time for deeper hopes. There is the hope for stronger family bonds, for more love and mutual support among neighbors and friends, for lives more enriched by precious human contact.

There is the hope that what began in that stable will really change lives, that men will really begin to love their enemies and bless and do good to and pray for them.

There is the hope that as mankind is elevated in the light

of Christ, there can actually come peace on earth, good will to men.

So far, the record isn't encouraging. In two thousand years since that holy night, there has hardly been peace on earth. The violence and terrorism, the family disintegration, the economic confusion, the drug abuse and moral decay and the terrifying new disease they spawned—all these demonstrate little progress of good will toward men.

But Christmas is hope. It is a time to reflect that, grim as our prospects seem today, this is nothing new. Grim, indeed, were the prospects of the shepherds huddled that night on the hills outside Bethlehem.

Palestine squirmed under the rule of a tyrannical, bloodthirsty Roman puppet, a ruler so depraved in his madness he would soon order the slaughter of all male infants.

In such a place at such a time, hollow indeed to those without hope must have sounded the message: "Fear not: for, behold, I bring you good tidings of great joy. . . . " (Luke 2:10.)

The world has always had its Herods, and always will until the end comes. But God can and does change human hearts. He can and does replace greed with compassion, hatred with love. Not for all men and at all times has such change come. But enough that mankind has always survived the Herods.

Of course, the outcome is more critical now, more immediate. For the first time, our generation has the technology to destroy civilization. There may not be time for the mills of the gods to grind slowly, for the goodness among mankind to gradually overcome the evil. Which is why it has never been more urgent for men to turn to God, to put their trust in His promise: "Peace I leave with you, my peace I give unto you. . . . Let not your heart be troubled, neither let it be afraid." (John 14:27.)

The shepherds who worshipped at the manger and those who similarly worship today share the blessed assurance that the final word will be that of God, not man.

That is the hope of Christmas.

HE WILL STAY

In a system of designation based on phases of the moon, Easter may fall as early as March 22 or as late as April 25. Merchants and chambers of commerce don't much like that system. Men have tried to change it. The League of Nations in 1923 called a conference to agree on a fixed date; the British Parliament passed a fixed-date act in 1928; the Vatican II Ecumenical Council in 1963 recommended a fixed date.

But agreement seems distant; the tradition of seventeen centuries is strong. And it is just as well, because there is profound, if unintended, symbolism in the way the date is set.

It was the Council of Nicea in 325 A.D. that set Easter on the first Sunday after the first full moon following the spring equinox. At that time, thousands of devout Christians were making pilgrimages to the Holy Land. The Easter policy was adopted to help them travel in safety by the light of the full moon.

Travelers don't need the light of the full moon today. But in a higher sense, we are all pilgrims. We all seek the Holy Land. In the effort to get there safely, we face dangers more sinister, in the eternal sense, than did those seeking to reach Jerusalem.

How desperately we need to make the journey in the Light of Christ. Two who learned to walk in that light we learn about in the 24th chapter of Luke. One was a disciple named Cleopas.

The other, judging by the immediacy and passion of the account, probably was Luke himself.

They had been in Jerusalem, apparently, during the terrible night and day of the Savior's betrayal, arrest, trial, and crucifixion. They had heard the perplexing reports of the two Marys and Peter and others about an empty tomb and angels saying He is risen. Like Peter, they had undoubtedly wondered at what had come to pass. Certainly they had not understood.

And now, later on that same day of resurrection, they set out from Jerusalem on the road to Emmaus, some seven and one-half miles away. Sad, confused, no doubt bitterly disappointed in the blighting of their hopes for a Redeemer, they could talk of nothing else than the events of those three days.

When the Risen Lord himself joined them along the way, their hearts were so turned inward to their own grief they did not know Him and poured out the story of how He who was to have redeemed Israel had, instead, been condemned and executed.

To such sorrowing, confused, ordinary human beings, the Resurrected Savior gave His first extensive teachings. Nor was it new doctrine He taught. Turning to the scriptures, He patiently explained how prophets since Moses had foretold the mission of the Messiah, His suffering, His resurrection.

At last, they began to understand. Their hearts began to burn with the conviction that leads men to total discipleship. When the village was reached and He would have left them, "they constrained Him, saying, Abide with us." And He stayed, even as, over and over, He has said . . . knock and it shall be opened . . . seek and ye shall find.

Now no longer a stranger, but the Master, He broke bread, blessed it, and gave to them. "And their eyes were opened, and they knew Him, and He vanished out of their sight."

He lives! Man shall live! There is no more vital, eternally meaningful, unspeakably joyful message than this.

But there is more: The truth that here and now, in this complex, challenging, risky pilgrimage on which we all have embarked, we ordinary men and women can walk by His light. He has given us the words of the prophets to help us know how to turn to that light. He has spoken to us peace. And, wonder of wonders, if we constrain Him, if we earnestly seek His presence, He will stay.

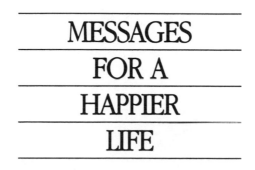

MESSAGES
FOR A
HAPPIER
LIFE

RISING ABOVE OURSELVES

In his insightful and provocative book *The Seven Mysteries of Life*, Guy Murchie describes a phenomenon in nature he calls social transcendence. When the individual consciousness is absorbed into and becomes part of a group consciousness, individual capabilities are transcended in astonishing ways.

Examples are many. One of the most dramatic is that of the carnivorous army ant. Individually, this ant is no match for other ants or many other insects. Individually, it behaves randomly, if not moronically. "But when a colony of thousands or (better) millions of ants is functioning," Murchie writes, "a definite intelligence is evident and the ants' activity becomes coordinated and purposeful, sometimes rising to the point of instinctive brilliance."

Marching by the millions in a column a yard or two wide, perhaps one hundred yards long, the army ant is invincible in the animal kingdom. Even elephants flee its approach. Pythons and crocodiles as well as smaller victims are killed and consumed in a matter of minutes. Facing hot coals, ants in the forward ranks sacrifice themselves, "creating with their thousands of bodies, an eventual causeway of ash the rest of the army can march over." To cross a stream, they will form a living bridge, clinging to each other to the death while the rest cross over. If the stream is too wide, they form themselves into "a kind of Noah's Ark, a roughly spherical vessel with enough enclosed air to float, and thus launch themselves as if with a single mind."

Colonies of termites act with a similar kind of group consciousness and intelligence. So do beehives. So do schools of certain kinds of fish and flocks of some birds. Individually, such creatures can hardly survive, much less act purposefully. Only as part of a group mind can they attain the purpose of their creation.

These simple examples may tell us something profound and divine about man's relationship with his fellow beings and with his Creator.

Some find it a hard doctrine that, as king Benjamin told his people, "the natural man is an enemy to God" (Mosiah 3:19), a person of "nothingness" in a "worthless and fallen state." (Mosiah 4:5.) We are sons and daughters of God, created in His image. How can we be nothing and worthless?

The nothingness of the army ant, acting in and of itself, may give a clue. Believing our own self-sufficiency, failing to yield ourselves to the mind and will of God, failing to acknowledge our dependence on Him and His redemptive sacrifice, failing to live His teachings, we are, in the eternal scheme of things, also worthless and purposeless.

King Benjamin's people learned that message. They believed his words "because of the Spirit of the Lord Omnipotent, which has wrought a mighty change in us, or in our hearts, that we have no more disposition to do evil, but to do good continually." (Mosiah 5:2.)

What an invincible force would be a society—a church—made up of individuals who had experienced that mighty change, who had united in the disposition only to do good, who had become one with the will of God. In such a society, our individual powers would be transcended here and, in ways beyond human comprehension, hereafter.

But, it may be objected, we are not ants. We possess God-given intelligence and are expected to use it, not submerge it in a group mind. What of our freedom if we yield our will to God's will?

Here is the great secret. True freedom is in voluntarily, intelligently choosing a higher realm of operation. When we experience the "mighty change" and lose the disposition to act carnally, we throw off the shackles tying us to carnal things. Having only the disposition to do good, how glorious would be our freedom to make our decisions in that realm.

King Benjamin spoke to his people, and us, of that freedom: "And now, because of the covenant which ye have made ye shall be called the children of Christ, his sons, and his daughters; for behold, this day he hath spiritually begotten you; for ye say that your hearts are changed through faith on his name; therefore, ye are born of him and have become his sons and his daughters.

"And under this head ye are made free, and there is no other head whereby ye can be made free." (Mosiah 5:7-8.)

THE ATTITUDE OF GRATITUDE

*What would you not pay to see the moon
rise if nature had not made it free entertain-
ment? (Richard Le Gallienne.)*

What, indeed, would one not pay for sunshine, for rain,
for a child's love, for sleep, for fingers that work, for each
new day, had all these blessings and infinitely more not been
freely given by a loving Heavenly Father?

Yet, how seldom we pause to give thanks for these everyday
things. How seldom are our souls suffused with awe and gratitude for the magnificence of His gifts.

How unthinkingly, how obtusely we take it all for granted.

Gratitude, Samuel Johnson said two centuries ago, is a fruit
of great cultivation; it is not found among gross people. If this
be true, it follows that an essential goal in our striving toward
perfection must be development of a lively and unfailing attitude of gratitude.

The Lord expects it of us. Over and over, the scriptures
enjoin us to give thanks in all things, to praise and thank God
without ceasing. His promise is great to those who do. If we
thank the Lord in all things, if we offer a broken heart and
contrite spirit, keep the Lord's day holy, and do these things
with thanksgiving, with glad hearts and cheerful countenances,
then the fullness of the earth is promised us, "all things which

come of the earth...to please the eye and gladden the heart...to strengthen the body and to enliven the soul."

But then comes the warning: "And in nothing doth man offend God, or against none is his wrath kindled, save those who confess not his hand in all things...." (D&C 59:21.)

Pride and arrogance the Lord hates. (See Prov. 8:13.) What greater pride is there than failure to acknowledge that all blessings come from God, what greater arrogance than failure to give thanks for them?

Essential along with an attitude of gratitude to God is a like attitude toward our fellow men. Gratitude is the lubricant in human affairs. The service we freely give to those we love, or to those we don't, would become drudgery and grind to a halt without it.

On the wall of a teenager's bedroom hangs a poster:

> Gratitude takes three forms
> A feeling in the heart
> An expression in words
> And a giving in return

He is happiest and comes closest to perfection who keeps the feeling of gratitude in his heart at all times, whatever happens to him. Depression and despair attack those who convince themselves that no one cares. That conviction is impossible for one who carries in his heart a feeling of gratitude to a loving Heavenly Father and to his fellowmen. Gratitude and depression cannot exist in the same mind at the same time. Gratitude in the heart blesses the one in whose heart it grows. Gratitude expressed in words blesses others as well.

The story is told of a group of men who were talking about people who had influenced their lives and to whom they were grateful. One man thought of a high school teacher who had introduced him to Tennyson. He decided to write and thank her.

In time, written in a feeble scrawl, came this letter:

"My dear Willie:

"I can't tell you how much your note meant to me. I am in my 80s living alone in a small room, cooking my own meals, lonely and like the last leaf lingering behind. You will be interested to know that I taught school for 50 years and yours is the first note of appreciation I have ever received. It came on a blue, cold morning and it cheered me as nothing has for years."

So little effort to express thanks. So greatly multiplied the effect. So it is in all human relationships — and in relationships with God.

As for giving in return, Edward Arlington Robinson spoke of

> Two kinds of gratitude; the sudden kind
> We feel for what we take, the larger kind
> We feel for what we give.

So it is. Gratitude felt and spoken ennobles the soul. Gratitude expressed in action, in giving, enlarges it as well.

READY FOR A CRASH LANDING

For two hours the airliner, its landing gear crippled, had circled over the Florida coast, dumping fuel. For two hours its passengers had prepared for the crash landing they knew was coming. Some prayed. Some wept. Some spoke quietly together of lives shared, of love given and received. Some, no doubt, anguished over deeds done or undone.

At last, the waiting was over. The time had come to live or die.

With the greatest care the pilot eased onto the runway at Miami airport. On its belly the giant jet skidded and bounced to a halt as fire trucks raced alongside, smothering with foam the fire that briefly erupted. Passengers tumbled down the emergency chutes and dashed for safety.

Foam-drenched and shaken, but safe, the passengers recounted their emotions and thoughts during the ordeal. A never-to-be-forgotten comment came from one of a group of LDS missionaries returning from Ecuador: "I resolved to live the rest of my life prepared for a crash landing."

That was in essence the Savior's urgent last message to His disciples before His last night on earth. Be ready for a crash landing. Be ready for the Lord's coming, or — more to the point for most of us — for our going.

He had just spoken (see Matt. 24) of the signs of His coming. He had warned that no man knew the hour or day, simply that

49

we should be ready. Then followed two of his most pointed parables (see Matt. 25), among the last He would give.

Eagerly, ten virgins, bridesmaids, awaited arrival of the bridegroom. Each had brought her lamp to light the wedding procession. Five had brought no oil, expecting, perhaps, to be provided from a common supply. The hour grew late. The bridesmaids slept. Suddenly, at midnight, the cry came, "The bridegroom cometh; go ye out to meet him."

Hastily, lamps were lit. Five, without oil, immediately went out. Their owners asked the others to share. No, they were told, they must provide their own. While they scrambled to do so, the bridegroom arrived, the door was shut, the five unprepared bridesmaids missed the wedding.

The meaning cannot be misunderstood. The bridegroom is the Lord, whose second coming has so long been awaited. The wedding is His Kingdom, the bridesmaids His disciples, the lamps the symbol of their discipleship, the oil the individual, personal preparation essential to make the lamp burn.

Each of us is responsible for his own oil. There can be no borrowing from others. There is no common supply. When the unknown day and hour arrive, it will be too late for last-minute preparation.

Caught short of oil, no matter how earnestly we profess discipleship, we are in danger of hearing those dreadful words: "I know you not."

How, then, must we provide the oil? The Lord's entire ministry was devoted to teaching and showing how. But the parable that immediately follows that of the Ten Virgins makes unmistakably clear what He expects of those who profess to follow Him.

The parable of the talents, the blessing of the servants who used and doubled their talents, the condemnation of the one who didn't, is generally — and properly — understood to mean that God expects us to use constructively the time, energy, and intelligence He has given us. If we do, these gifts will be increased. If we don't, they will be lost.

But to His disciples, the meaning is more specific. They were *His own servants* whom the Master had called. They were *His* goods with which He entrusted them before leaving for a "far country."

The Lord has left to be with His Father. He has left His kingdom in the hands of His servants. To some He has entrusted five talents, some two, some one. Some are called as General Authorities, some as bishops, some as stake missionaries, some as home or visiting teachers.

For all, the expectation is the same: Magnify the calling. Proclaim the gospel. Perfect the saints. Redeem the dead. Return to the Lord, when He returns, His kingdom enlarged and strengthened and perfected.

To those who do, who come to the wedding with their own oil, will He say: "Well done, thou good and faithful servant: thou hast been faithful over a few things, I will make thee ruler over many things: enter thou into the joy of thy lord." (Matt. 25:21.)

THE SEARCH FOR HAPPINESS

In a quiet New England churchyard lies a headstone whose epitaph contains a profoundly important message — a goal — for all of us:

> Here lies a woman twice blessed;
> She was happy, and she knew it.

Twice blessed, indeed. Happiness is the proper pursuit of mankind. Man is that he might have joy. All we do should be directed toward that goal.

But for most of us, unlike the woman in that New England grave, the pursuit of happiness is complicated by not knowing when we have found it. So we anxiously wait for happiness to come at some future time. We will be happy when we are old enough to drive a car, when we get married, when we have children, when we buy the new house, when we get that big promotion and can buy a bigger house in a better neighborhood, when the children are on their own and we can get some peace, when we are retired and can travel and do the things we've never had time to do. Then we will be happy.

And, suddenly, we find ourselves looking back and remembering when we were happy and wishing we could be there again.

So many of us think we can find happiness when times are "normal" — when the economy is better and the stock market settles down, when we no longer live under threat of nuclear war, when we have achieved order and normality in our own lives.

But times were never "normal." They never will be. What we see is what we have. Today is as "normal" as it is going to get. A discouraging thought? Yes, for those who can't come to grips with and apply in their lives the truth that happiness is a state of mind. It is within. It has nothing to do with "the times."

With that truth, we can abandon our pursuit of externalities leading to happiness. We can quiet our souls. We can take to heart the counsel of Nathaniel Hawthorne: "Happiness is . . . a butterfly which when pursued is just beyond your grasp but . . . if you will sit down quietly, may alight upon you."

Are we then to be passive about this matter of happiness? Is there nothing we should be doing about this most important goal of human existence? Of course not. We have only to learn whence happiness really comes, and live our lives accordingly. As we learn, we will find that every true source of happiness calls not for frenetic searching but for quiet consistency.

As always, the place to learn is the scriptures, the word of God.

The first key is righteousness. Wickedness never was happiness, Alma warns. (See Alma 41:10.) If there be no righteousness there be no happiness, Nephi affirms. (See 2 Ne. 2:13.) And the work of righteousness shall be peace; and the effect of righteousness quietness and assurance for ever. (See Isa. 32:17.) Peace, quietness, assurance; that's certainly the foundation for happiness.

But there are other stones in the foundation, perhaps less widely recognized. Happy is the man who finds wisdom, Proverbs tells us (3:13), and who has mercy on the poor (14:21), who keeps the law (29:18), and who trusts in the Lord (16:20). No externalities here; all these sources of happiness are within.

So is that supremely important essential for happiness—

appropriate self-esteem. Paul spells it out succinctly: Happy is he that condemneth not himself. (See Rom. 14:22.)

James adds another essential: We count them happy which endure. (See James 5:11.) And Alma still another—that we be truly penitent. (See Alma 27:18.)

But it was the Savior Himself who gave the most challenging and profound key of all. After giving His disciples the most poignant example of self-effacing service and challenging them to follow, He promised: "If ye know these things, happy are ye if ye do them." (John 13:17.)

Isn't that what life's experience teaches us—that it is when we lose ourselves in the service of others we find our greatest joy?

HARBOR OF FORGIVENESS

To some it may seem strange to see ships of many nations loading and unloading cargo along the docks at Portland, Oregon. That city is one hundred miles from the ocean. Getting there involves a difficult, often turbulent passage over the bar guarding the Columbia River and a long trip up the Columbia and Willamette rivers.

But ship captains like to tie up at Portland. They know that as their ships travel the seas, a curious saltwater shellfish called a barnacle fastens itself to the hull and stays there for the rest of its life, surrounding itself with a rocklike shell. As more and more barnacles attach themselves, they increase the ship's drag, slow its progress, decrease its efficiency.

Periodically, the ship must go into dry dock, where with great effort the barnacles are chiseled and scraped off. It's a difficult, expensive process that ties up the ship for days.

But not if the captain can get his ship to Portland. Barnacles can't live in fresh water. There, in the sweet, fresh waters of the Willamette or Columbia, the barnacles loosen and fall away, and the ship returns to its task lightened and renewed.

Sins are like those barnacles. Hardly anyone goes through life without picking up some. They increase the drag, slow our progress, decrease our efficiency. Unrepented, building up one on another, they can eventually sink us.

In His infinite love and mercy, our Lord has provided a

harbor where, through repentance, our barnacles fall away and are forgotten. With our souls lightened and renewed, we can go efficiently about our work and His. Through His atonement comes an endless, abundant flood of grace. Sin can't live in that sweet water. But we have to make the effort, through repentance, to get there, and the trip can be difficult and turbulent.

That's what Lehi, nearing the end of his life, was trying to tell his sons. To Jacob he promised: " . . . thy days shall be spent in the service of thy God. Wherefore, I know that thou art redeemed, because of the righteousness of thy Redeemer; for thou hast beheld that in the fulness of time he cometh to bring salvation unto men.

" . . . And the way is prepared from the fall of man, and salvation is free.

"And men are instructed sufficiently that they know good from evil. And the law is given unto men. And by the law no flesh is justified; or, by the law men are cut off. Yea, by the temporal law they were cut off; and also, by the spiritual law they perish from that which is good, and become miserable forever.

"Wherefore, redemption cometh in and through the Holy Messiah; for he is full of grace and truth.

"Behold, he offereth himself a sacrifice for sin, to answer the ends of the law, unto all those who have a broken heart and a contrite spirit; and unto none else can the ends of the law be answered." (2 Ne. 2:3-7.)

Salvation is free. From the beginning, from the fall, the way was prepared for the Savior's atoning sacrifice to break the bands of death for all men.

But there is a law. Men were taught it, were taught to know good from evil, were given the freedom to choose. Our Savior is a God of justice and of mercy. By law is justice served. By His atonement we receive mercy, available to all in an unfailing flood. But, by the law, only by crossing the bar of repentance, by coming with broken heart and contrite spirit, can we shed our barnacles in the waters of His atoning grace. Those who don't, remain miserable forever.

To those who do cleanse themselves and live as the Lord taught, in virtue and with Christian love to all men, comes the greatest of all promises: Confidence in the presence of God. (See D&C 121:45.)

ARE WE REALLY FREE?

Free agency is the gospel's cornerstone. Without it, the Savior's redeeming sacrifice and the plan of salvation itself, would be meaningless.

The scriptures on freedom are convincing: "And ye shall know the truth, and the truth shall make you free." (John 8:32.) "Stand fast therefore in the liberty wherewith Christ hath made us free...." (Gal. 5:1.) "...Behold, ye are free; ye are permitted to act for yourselves; for behold, God hath given unto you a knowledge and he hath made you free." (Hel. 14:30.)

But there is a problem here, or seems to be. What of those who don't have the truth? What of those who never heard of Christ or the knowledge He gave? What of the billions of people who struggle for existence against starvation and disease in the dark places of the earth — or, indeed, those in our "modern" nations who are trapped in crime-ridden pockets of poverty, ignorance, and despair? What, in fact, of ordinary people living ordinary lives suddenly overwhelmed by crises or tragedy not of their own making?

Are these people really free? Are they not hopelessly trapped by what is happening to them?

Dominique LaPierre in his book *City of Joy* suggests an answer. He describes the desperation of life in Calcutta's leprous, starvation-ridden slums. And then he writes: "In these slums people actually put love and mutual support into practice. They know how to be tolerant of all creeds and castes, how to give respect to a stranger, how to show charity toward beggars, cripples, lepers and even the insane. Here the weak were helped, not trampled upon. Orphans were instantly adopted by their neighbors, and old people were cared for and revered by their children."

The Jewish psychiatrist Victor Frankl examines this question of freedom. In his book *Man's Search for Meaning* he describes his life in Nazi concentration camps, where his father, mother, brother, and wife perished in the gas ovens.

And he asks: "What about human liberty? Is there no spiritual freedom in regard to behavior and reaction to any given surroundings? Is that theory true which would have us believe that man is no more than a product of many conditional and environmental factors—be they of a biological, psychological or sociological nature?"

His answer is unequivocal: "Man *can* preserve a vestige of spiritual freedom, of independence of mind, even in such terrible conditions of psychic and physical stress.

"We who lived in concentration camps can remember the men who walked through the huts comforting others, giving away their last piece of bread. They may have been few in number, but they offer sufficient proof that everything can be taken from a man but one thing: the last of the human freedoms—to choose one's attitude in any given set of circumstances, to choose one's own way."

As a further witness, hear the apostle Paul. Near the end of his ministry, times were tough for Paul. Writing to the saints in Corinth, he described his personal ordeal: Five times scourged with the thirty-nine lashes that sometimes killed the victim; three times beaten with rods, once stoned, three times shipwrecked, constantly imperiled by robbers, by his own countrymen as well as by heathen, by the wilderness, by the sea, by false brethren.

Nor was he alone. Stephen had died a martyr. So had others. So, soon, would Paul.

In these conditions, this was his testimony: "We are troubled on every side, yet not distressed; we are perplexed, but not in despair;

"Persecuted, but not forsaken; cast down, but not destroyed. . . .

"For our light affliction, which is but for a moment, worketh for us a far more exceeding and eternal weight of glory;

"While we look not at the things which are seen, but at the things which are not seen: for the things which are seen are temporal; but the things which are not seen are eternal." (2 Cor. 4:8-9, 17-18.)

Man *is* free. His true freedom has nothing to do with his place of birth, his economic or social or educational status, the vagaries of man or even of nature.

Freedom is given by God. It is within. No outward force can destroy it. Whether in a Calcutta slum, a Nazi concentration camp, on the wrong end of a scourging, or in any of the vicissitudes of modern life, man is free to choose—either to surrender, or to live the dignity and integrity of Christ-seeking humanity.

THE FIRST COMMANDMENT

When Moses came down from the smoke and fire of Sinai, the tablets he bore proclaimed as God's first commandment: Thou shalt have no other gods before me. The second, third, and fourth amplified that theme — things like making no graven images, not taking God's name in vain, keeping His sabbath holy.

Not until the last half of the list do we get the practical rules to govern our conduct. And then we are told in the briefest possible terms not to kill, commit adultery, steal, bear false witness, covet.

That seems curious. Why aren't the Ten Commandments given in order of importance?

The answer, of course, is that they are. All other commandments rest on the first. God is truth, love, justice, mercy. Worshipping any other god, putting any other value — wealth, power, fame, pleasure — before Him, is the worst kind of idolatry. No other commandment would be necessary if we obeyed the first.

Pride is the commonest and most pernicious form of idolatry. It lies at the root of all the other forms. When we rely on our own strength, our own wisdom, our own abilities, when we fail to acknowledge our dependence on God, we are putting another god before Him. Few if any among us are entirely guiltless.

61

Pride has been called the Nephite disease. Throughout the Book of Mormon, their history repeats; when they humbly worshipped God, they prospered. But again and again, they put other gods first. Again and again they were raised up in the pride of self-sufficiency, with all the evils attendant to such an attitude. Each time they suffered, and ultimately they were destroyed.

You'd think they would learn. It's hard to comprehend why they didn't—until we realize that the Lord's warnings about the idolatry of pride are intended for our day as well, and that many of us don't listen any better than did the Nephites.

It was 2,500 years ago that, through Nephi, the warning came, but the message is as modern as today: " . . . and their priests shall contend one with another, and they shall teach with their learning and deny the Holy Ghost . . . And they deny the power of God, the Holy One of Israel; and they say unto the people . . . behold there is no God today, for the Lord and the Redeemer hath done his work, and he hath given his power unto men; . . .

"O the wise, and the learned, and the rich, that are puffed up in the pride of their hearts, . . . at that day shall he [Satan] rage in the hearts of the children of men, and stir them up to anger against that which is good. And others will he pacify, and lull them away into carnal security, that they will say: All is well in Zion; yea, Zion prospereth, all is well—and thus the devil cheateth their souls, and leadeth them away carefully down to hell. . . .

"Wo be unto him that shall say: We have received the word of God, and we need no more of the word of God, for we have enough! . . .

"Cursed is he that putteth his trust in man, or maketh flesh his arm, or shall hearken unto the precepts of men. . . . "(2 Ne. 28:4-5, 15, 20, 29, 31.)

Why did our Savior teach so eloquently and repeatedly the importance of humility? Why did He Himself set such an example? Because He knew the first commandment. Pride in our wisdom and learning, in our wealth, in the flesh of our arms must never blind us to our dependence on God.

The truth is that the work of our Lord and Redeemer is far from finished. He accomplished His part of the divine mission in Gethsemane and on the cross, but that didn't complete the Atonement. For each of us, there is no atonement until we take upon ourselves His name, keep His commandments, and perfect ourselves in Him.

In pride, we can never accomplish these things. No one can stand in His presence but through His grace. Until we truly obey the first commandment, we cannot return to Him.

THE LOAN OF LIFE

A thunderstorm with its deadly windshears. A light plane attempting to land. A sudden, terrible gust, and a family of five is dead, including a man and his wife, their son, daughter-in-law, and grandchild.

Surviving family members struggle to understand. So do officers and employees of companies this man had founded and fostered. So do many in business, government, and education who had looked to him for leadership. So do friends who had loved this family for its generous goodness, and who feel deeply the loss.

Comfort and sympathy are freely expressed. Explanations are attempted. But who knows the mind and purpose of God? In the end, the wise among us accept the message expressed on a plaque hanging on the wall of a venerable family doctor:

> It has taken all my life for me to understand
> that I don't need to understand everything.

What we do understand, and are reminded of almost any time we pick up the daily paper, is that life is tenuous. It can end without warning, and had better be lived fully and responsibly and productively—as this family certainly lived theirs—while there is time.

A four-word phrase in king Benjamin's address to his people makes the unforgettable point: "I say unto you that if ye should serve him who has created you from the beginning, and is preserving you from day to day, *by lending you breath*, that ye may live and move and do according to your own will, and even supporting you from one moment to another—I say, if ye should serve him with all your whole souls yet ye would be unprofitable servants." (Mosiah 2:21; italics added.)

By lending you breath; what an insightful key to the mystery of mortal existence. Our bodies, our minds, our abilities, our very breath are on loan from our Creator.

There are certain things about loans that we all understand. One is that this kind of loan can be called at any time, at the lender's will, without recourse or argument or explanation. That's the condition on which we accept the loan. If it's called earlier than expected, sorrow is appropriate, but certainly not bitterness or feelings of injustice.

Another is that we are expected to return the loaned object in good condition, excepting normal wear and tear. Those who say, "It's *my* body, and no one can tell me what to do with it," don't understand. It isn't their body. It's a loan. To damage it carelessly is irresponsible and shameful.

A third thing about loans is that there's an interest charge attached. The lender expects a profit. He expects us to improve our talents, not bury them. He expects service to our fellow men as the interest we pay. It's true that the loan is so magnificent that, no matter how hard we try, what we repay can't possibly represent profitable interest by earthly standards. But the Lord's bookkeeping isn't based on earthly standards.

In His unimaginable generosity, ". . . all that he requires of you is to keep his commandments . . . [and] if ye do keep his commandments he doth bless you and prosper you." (Mosiah 2:22.)

RAISE YOUR THERMOSTAT

In the Northern Hemisphere on wintry days, a device hanging unobstrusively on the wall in most homes determines, to a large extent, our physical comfort.

It's called a thermostat, and is a marvel of efficient simplicity.

Set one pointer at a certain level and it turns on the heating system when the temperature falls to that level. Set the other pointer a few degrees higher and it shuts off when the heat reaches that level.

The range of temperature between those two points is called the comfort zone. Someone in authority determines what the comfort zone should be — usually after considerable prompting — and sets the thermostat. There it stays, faithfully keeping the temperature in that range — until someone else overrules the someone in authority and sets it higher. Which, in the home we know best, usually comes sooner than later.

There is within each of us a thermostat that governs our performance. It's called self-image. Each of us determines who and what we are and sets the thermostat accordingly. When we get outside the comfort zone we set for ourselves, it creates tensions and we correct our behavior to get back where our self-image tells us we belong.

"As [a man] thinketh in his heart, so is he." (Prov. 23:7.) We are what we think — or, rather, feel — we are. The only way we can achieve lasting, productive change in our lives is to change the way we feel about ourselves.

Around the first of the year, there's a lot of resolution-making. We resolve to perform better in our jobs, abandon sin, be more energetic, lose weight, treat our spouses better. But all that resolving is useless if we still think of ourselves as inefficient, sinful, lazy, fat, or mean.

We must reset the thermostat. But how?

If we fully understood — and lived — the gospel, we would have no trouble with self-image. How could we, knowing that we are sons and daughters of God, made in His image, having within us the potential of godhood? How could we doubt our worth as individuals, knowing we are so worthwhile, in God's eyes, that His entire plan of salvation, His work and glory, His gift of His Only Begotten Son, are to bring to pass our eternal life? Knowing this, having low self-esteem is a form of blasphemy.

The trouble is, we don't *act* like sons and daughters of God. We sin. We fall short of His hopes and expectations. We feel guilt, and guilt keeps us from feeling good about ourselves.

That is when it is most important to stay in touch with Him. That is when searching study of the scriptures and searching prayer are most essential, to be assured by His word that we are His children, that He loves us, that we are worthy of His love, that because we are worthy He has given the great gift of repentance with the promise that if we repent, our sins will be wiped away, that He will remember them no more.

If God remembers not our weaknesses, we must forget them, too. Forget our crooked teeth or halting speech or lack of confidence around others. Forget all our weaknesses and emphasize our strengths. Forget our failures and remember our successes. Know that we can succeed, because we have succeeded.

It is told of the painter Whistler that he once created a tiny painting of a spray of roses. The artistry was so superb that it was the envy of artists who saw it, the despair of collectors who yearned to buy it. But Whistler refused to sell, saying, "Whenever I feel that my hand has lost its cunning, whenever I doubt my ability, I look at that little painting and say to myself, 'Whistler, you painted that. Your hand drew it. Your imagination conceived the colors. Your skill put the roses on the canvas.' Then I know that what I have done, I can do again."

Like Whistler, let us hang on the walls of our minds the memory of our successes. Take counsel of our strength, not our weakness. Remember the big moments, the times we have risen above our comfort zone, and know that what we have done we can do again. And again.

"Neglect not the gift that is in thee," the apostle Paul exhorted his young disciple Timothy—and each of us. "For God has not given us the spirit of fear; but of power, and of love, and of a sound mind." (1 Tim. 4:14; 2 Tim. 1:7.)

Power. Love. Sound mind. This is how God sees us. Can we not so see ourselves, reset our self-esteem thermostat at a higher level, and perform as God intended?

FIVE ANTENNAE FOR HEARING GOD

Prayer keeps a man from sin, Brigham Young once said, and sin keeps a man from prayer.

It's true. The scriptures are full of the assurance that prayer is the first and best defense against the powers of the destroyer. "Humble yourself before the Lord," Alma pleaded, "and call on his holy name, and watch and pray continually, that ye may not be tempted above that which ye can bear." (Alma 13:28.)

Sin can clog the communication lines to heaven. The soul darkened with unrepented sin is in no condition to get a message through. Mark Twain knew about that. His Huckleberry Finn described the condition of far too many of us: "I about made up my mind to pray and see if I couldn't try to quit bein' the kind of boy I was and be better. So I kneeled down. But the words wouldn't come. Why wouldn't they? It weren't no use to try and hide it from Him. . . . I knowed very well why they wouldn't come. It was because my heart wasn't right; it was because I was playin' double. I was lettin' on to give up sin, but way inside of me I was holdin' on to the biggest one of all. I was tryin' to make my mouth say I would do the right thing and the clean thing, but deep down in me I knowed it was a lie and He knowed it. You can't pray a lie."

But it's not just sin that keeps us from prayer. It's also indifference or laziness. Effective communication with God takes hard, concentrated effort. Too often, we make prayer a matter of convenience instead of high priority for our time and attention.

And often, it's lack of faith — real faith that He will hear and answer — that makes our effort superficial, if we make the effort at all. We haven't recognized a clear answer to our prayers, or it has been a while and we've forgotten. The Lord must have known how quickly we forget, which is why He pleaded with us to pray evening, and morning, and at noon (see Ps. 55:17), to pray without ceasing (see 2 Thes. 5:17), to call on the name of the Lord daily (see Mosiah 4:11), to let our hearts be full, drawn out in prayer unto him continually (see Alma 34:27).

Or it's that we don't recognize answers when they come. We pray, but don't listen. Or we don't listen long and patiently enough. Jesus' plea (Matt. 24:42) to watch, "for ye know not what hour your Lord doth come" applies not only to His second coming, but also to those times in the life of each of us when quietly He comes in answer to our prayers.

As we listen for the answer, we may well reflect on how it may come. It may come directly, powerfully, immediately recognizable, of course. But it may come subtly, knowable only to the sensitive, listening heart.

In his luminous little book, *He Touched Me; My Pilgrimage of Prayer*, John Powell suggests five quiet ways in which God may answer prayer: "Can God put a new idea directly and immediately into my *mind?* Can God put new desires into my *heart*, new strength into my will? Can He touch and calm my turbulent *emotions?* Can He actually whisper words to the listening ears of my soul through the inner faculty of my *imagination?* Can God stimulate certain *memories* stored within the human brain at the time these memories are needed?

"If the answer to these questions is yes, then God has at least five channels through which He can reach me, five antennae in my human anatomy through which He can 'touch' me.... I feel sure that God can and does reach us in these ways.... God is available and anxious to speak to you and me. Yes, just as anxious as he was to speak to Abraham, Isaac and Jacob, Isaiah and Jeremiah."

70

LIGHT IN DARK PLACES

The day was dark. Clouds lowered over the higher peaks as the highway climbed the canyon. But autumn made the world beautiful. Maple reds and oranges splashed the lower slopes. Higher, pockets of golden aspen gleamed among the dark conifers.

"Isn't it interesting," someone remarked. "Where those aspen are, it looks like the sun is shining."

So it is in human affairs. Where one individual, or a few, glows with the light of Christ, no matter how dark the day or the time, it looks like the sun is shining. If the glow is bright enough and lasts long enough, sooner or later it will shine.

The young mother stood in front of her house, her year-old baby in her arms, warming in the morning sun. Idly, she watched three planes approach from the south. She glanced at her watch: 8:15. Time to fix breakfast for the children and her mother and sister. But just a few minutes more in the sun.

The day: August 6, 1945. The place: Hiroshima.

Yoshiko Nakamura never felt the cataclysm that blasted her into unconsciousness. Neither did her baby; it died instantly. So did her mother and sister. Seventy thousand others died in that instant and the days of agony that followed. Her two-year-old son lived thirty-three days and died from burns, her husband ten years later from radiation.

Her own body was badly burned. "For three years, I had

71

no hair," she recalled. "My teeth hurt so I couldn't eat solid food for a year. My legs were so full of splinters I couldn't walk for three months."

Dark times, dark places. But the light of Christ can make it seem like the sun is shining.

"Four months after my husband died, the missionaries came to my door," she recalled. "I understood their message and was baptized. I have been so happy."

Twenty-five years later, that bereaved mother had been several times Relief Society president of the Hiroshima Branch. "All these are my family now," she said, indicating fifty or so branch members and investigators leaving the tiny chapel. She had cared for their sick, helped bury their dead, taught them to be better mothers, helped them learn the gospel, as Relief Society presidents have done the world over.

Her glow and that of others like her were strong enough and long enough that the sun broke through and shines bright today. Where 70,000 bodies once lay in the rubble of a ruined city, a stake of the Church prospers, as do twenty-two others throughout the country that was once a hated enemy.

That's primarily how the gospel spreads — through the glow of people. The Holy Ghost does the converting, of course. But the Holy Ghost seldom gets a chance until the potential convert has first been attracted by someone — a missionary, a neighbor, a fellow worker, a schoolmate — who is following the Savior's injunction to "Let your light so shine before men that they may see your good works, and glorify your Father which is in heaven." (Matt. 5:16.)

What is it that makes a man or a woman glow? A noted expert on personal and corporate behavior lists such attributes as self-esteem, a sense of responsibility, optimism, imagination, awareness, creativity, joyfulness, trust.

These are helpful. But it's simpler than that. The apostle Paul gave the ultimate formula for glowing, no matter how dark the place: "And now abideth faith, hope, charity, these three; but the greatest of these is charity." (1 Cor. 13:13.)

By charity, the commentaries and other translations make clear, is meant pure love—love that suffers long and is kind, that has no room for envy, is not easily provoked, that thinks no evil but rejoices in the truth, that bears all things, hopes all things, endures all things.

Most of us are blessed to know a few—not many—people like that. In them we see a glow that seems to let sunshine into the dark places in their lives and our lives. In them we see light that, shining, leads others nearer to God.

LIVING FOR THE GIFTS

S ome years ago, the newswires reported the death of a Missouri minister after a fast of forty days. In papers found after his death he revealed his purpose: "I am seeking the more perfect will of God for my own life, and asking God to show me why the gifts of the spirit do not follow my ministry as Jesus said they would."

The gifts of the spirit — precious enough that one man died in search of them. How precious are they to us today?

Nearly a century ago, President George Q. Cannon spoke these blunt, challenging words to the saints: "How many of you . . . are seeking for these gifts that God has promised to bestow? How many of you, when you bow before your Heavenly Father in your family circle or in your secret places, contend for these gifts to be bestowed upon you? How many of you ask the Father, in the name of Jesus, to manifest Himself to you through these powers and these gifts? Or do you go along day by day like a door turning on its hinges, without having any feeling upon the subject, without exercising any faith whatever; content to be baptized and be members of the Church, and to rest there, thinking that your salvation is secure because you have done this? . . .

"God is the same today as He was yesterday . . . [He] is willing to bestow these gifts upon His children. I know that God is willing to heal the sick, that He is willing to bestow the gift of discerning of spirits, the gift of wisdom, of knowledge and of prophecy, and other gifts that may be needed." (*Millennial Star*, April 23, 1894, p. 260.)

These, and others, are the gifts of the Holy Ghost promised in 1 Corinthians chapter 12, Moroni chapter 10, and Doctrine and Covenants, section 46. How precious they are, these gifts of wisdom and knowledge and discernment, of faith to heal and be healed, of miracles and prophecy and tongues.

How eternally precious, especially, is that greatest of gifts, the knowledge that Jesus Christ is the Son of God, the Savior of the world.

But the gifts of the Spirit are not limited even to these. Paul opened a broader vision. In what may have been the last of his great epistles, written from a Roman dungeon from which he would soon walk to his death, he exhorted his young disciple, Timothy, to: " . . . stir up the gift of God, which is in thee by the putting on of my hands. For God hath not given us the spirit of fear; but of power, and of love, and of a sound mind." (2 Tim. 1:6-7.)

With such a testimony from such a man in such circumstances, who can deny man's responsibilities as spelled out in discomfiting clarity by President Cannon:

"If any of us are imperfect, it is our duty to pray for the gift that will make us perfect. Have I imperfections? I am full of them. What is my duty? To pray to God to give me the gifts that will correct these imperfections. If I am an angry man, it is my duty to pray for charity, which suffereth long and is kind. Am I an envious man? It is my duty to seek for charity, which envieth not. So with all the gifts of the Gospel. They are intended for this purpose. No man ought to say, 'Oh, I cannot help this; it is my nature.' He is not justified in it, for the reason that God has promised to give strength to correct these things, and to give gifts that will eradicate them." (Ibid.)

God does not expect us, like the fasting preacher of the Ozarks, to die in search of His gifts. He expects us to do something far more important. He expects us to live in search of them.

THE TIME TO CHANGE IS NOW

A special expectancy charged the congregation as the speaker approached the pulpit. Here was a much-respected man who for many years had not affiliated with the Church. Only recently had his life changed. The rejoicing over his return was still fresh. What, now, would be his message?

"By this hour next week," he began, "we will have observed a new year. Tradition has it that we make resolutions and make changes for the better at the beginning of a new year."

Appreciative nods. This man, surely, was qualified to talk of new beginnings and changes for the better.

He continued to explain that we have come to give special significance to certain times for changing, for starting or stopping things. But we should be ready and eager to do differently, to improve, *at any time*.

"We could decide at any moment to settle some difference, to do some service, to break a bad habit, to do better, to learn better, to live better. Such decision need not be left to a special day, a special hour, or a particular time in the future.

"And if we pass a particular time for improving or repenting, or if we falter or fail after having made a good resolution, we need not postpone the act of repentance or improvement for another special day, or hour, or another such season. The resolve to change should be *a continuous process,*

76

with frequent reminders, perhaps, but not with needless dramatics. A simple, quiet consistency serves best."

Then came what many had been anxious to hear — the account of what had turned around the life of this good man.

"Shortly after the return of my son Greg from his mission a small sign appeared on the refrigerator door:

'Be careful how you act.
'You may be the only Standard Work people read.'

"The sign appeared without fanfare. It has never been mentioned in my presence. It resides to this day in its place at the top of the refrigerator door — a quiet, frequent, consistent reminder.

"My son Greg knew it was quite possible that I might not ever read the Book of Mormon. But he knew quite certainly that I would read the language of his daily conduct. I read the pages of his life as he wrote them. It became my desire to be with him more often and to share his experience more fully. Eventually this desire led me to read the Book of Mormon."

Then followed his convincing testimony of the truth of the Book of Mormon, of the Savior's Sonship, of the missions of past and present Church presidents as His prophets.

"That these things are true," he testified, "I came to learn slowly through a process that began with my son's resolution to be careful how he acted."

In this simple, eloquent message are the essential elements of living successfully:

First, so live that others seeing your good works may glorify your Father which is in Heaven. What a joy for a son to know he has done that for his father.

Second, to know the truth, turn to the source of truth, the scriptures — in this case, especially the Book of Mormon.

Third, when a change is needed, do it. Do it now. Don't wait for New Year's resolutions or some other time based on custom or calendar.

Wisely, Lin Yutang counseled us about that:

"As we review our New Year's resolutions, we find we have fulfilled one-third of them, left unfilled another third, and can't remember what the other third was."

We should expect of ourselves better than one-third performance. Surely the Lord expects more. To help us achieve it, He gave one of His greatest gifts, repentance, and with it a total absence of restrictions as to time and place.

GET RID OF EXCUSES

Promise yourself that you will never, never make excuses for your poor performance. If somebody asks what your score is after a round, tell them your score. Don't tell them you got a bad lie in the rough.

"Never talk about a three putt, never talk about a bad break. Even if it wasn't your fault, say you played it as well as you could. People will respect you and you will respect yourself and in time you will play better.

"The only way to improve is to get rid of the excuses."

The speaker was Keith Clearwater at a youth golf camp at Brigham Young University. With good reason, the youngsters listened. Early in a professional career after being a golf all-American at BYU, Clearwater had just set a course record in the U.S. Open.

For an hour, he held his young audience spellbound with talk of life on the tour, golf swings, strategy. But in the process, he gave some profound truths that apply far beyond the bounds of a golf course.

On handling pressure: The only way to combat fear and pressure is to fill your mind with what you want to accomplish. Period. Positive thinking is filling your mind with what you want to do.

On fundamentals: Talk to Jack Nicklaus. He's the greatest who ever played the game. And all he does is improve his fundamentals. There are no secrets, no shortcuts. You just have to learn the basics and then build a game around them.

On character: These golf camps help you learn about golf, but it is your character that determines if you will be a winner.

On companions: Associate yourself with winners and people who are good.

But especially that advice about excuses. Clearwater put in simple, clear terms what behavior experts have been trying for years to tell us—and what the Lord Himself taught. One essential quality of a high-performance person is that of accepting accountability for his own acts. Every man and woman of real achievement has that quality in common, and with it the great feeling of guiding one's own destiny.

So many people go through life by the rule: "If at first you don't succeed, fix the blame fast." These are the people who never really grow up; the surest test of maturity is that of being comfortable with accountability. Only by accountability, by not making excuses, not blaming others, is progress possible.

There are, of course, things beyond our control. We are not responsible for earthquakes. We are not responsible, usually, for the mean or selfish acts of others. But we are responsible for our reaction to them. Accepting that responsibility is the mark of maturity, the key to progress.

The Lord left no room for doubt about our accountability. He will render to every man according to his deeds. (See Rom. 2:6.) And that's not all. In the day of judgment He will require an account of every idle word we speak. "For by thy words thou shalt be justified, and by thy words thou shalt be condemned." (See Matt. 12:36-37.)

And in our own time: " . . . every man may act in doctrine and principle pertaining to futurity, according to the moral agency which I have given unto him, that every man may be accountable for his own sins in the day of judgment." (D&C 101:78.)

What those youngsters heard in that golf camp may or may not help them hit a golf ball better. What it will surely do, if they really *heard*, is prepare them better for eternity.

MESSAGES
FOR THE
FAMILY

A BOUQUET EVERY DAY

Our neighbor around the block is known as the best gardener in our end of town. A special understanding seems to exist between her and her plants that enables her to coax them into glorious bloom at precisely the right time for her garden parties and other special events. While the rest of us fight aphids and mildew and the August blahs, her garden goes on and on blessing or comforting or gladdening every home within reach of her generous spirit.

For a long time, we had wanted to ask what her secret was. Finally we did. She came by during one of our infrequent but determined efforts to whip the garden into shape, grimly pinching back straggly petunias, pruning wilted rose blooms, staking sagging dahlias. When she stopped to chat, we straightened an aching back and asked right out: "How do you do it?"

Instead of some profound and technical explanation about soil and acidity or seeds and plant selection, or possibly something about planting in the right phase of the moon, the response was simple: "You just pick a bouquet every day."

"Oh, I see," we nodded, without the faintest idea what she was talking about.

Patiently, she explained. "Many days I don't need a bouquet. Some days I don't want one. Sometimes I don't feel like getting into the garden. But I have disciplined myself to make a new flower arrangement every single day.

"What it does is this: It makes the flowers feel wanted. It means I cut them when they are at their loveliest, not simply trimming off wilted blooms. They seem to appreciate this and put out a special effort. When I cut flowers daily, none of the plants gets straggly or goes to seed." She glanced at our pile of prunings and dead flower heads, but was kind enough not to press the point.

"What's more," she went on, "it keeps me close to the garden. I see each day what the flowers are doing. I recognize those that are struggling and I plan a way to help them. I spot trouble symptoms. When you are selecting and cutting flowers every day, you see the weeds and pull them out early. You see the aphids and the snails and the cutworms, and you keep them under control.

"But the main thing is, to enjoy the garden; it's amazing how much better flowers do when somebody enjoys and appreciates them."

As she walked on down the street, her words remained: Flowers do so much better when someone enjoys and appreciates them. And so, we thought, do people.

What if, in our relations with our children, we picked a bouquet every day? What if every day we made a special point of enjoying their talents, the warmth of a hug, the closeness of a private talk about things of special meaning to them?

What if we stayed close enough and interested enough, every day, to recognize the trouble spots early? What if instead of the periodic and inevitable confrontations, lectures, and discipline to cut back accumulated bad habits and enforce conformity—with all the trauma and alienation such confrontations produce—we handled these things gently and lovingly day by day?

What if every day our children knew—really knew—we enjoy and appreciate them? How much better might they do?

It's a heavy responsibility parents have been given in bringing children into the world and rearing them to responsible adulthood. The scriptures are full of exhortations to good parenthood and warnings to those who fail to make the effort.

Meeting the challenge has never been easy. Meeting it today, when families are so fragmented and destructive pressures are so great, is perhaps harder than it has ever been. Volumes have been written on how to do it. One widely quoted book on child care came to this conclusion:

"The more people have studied different methods of bringing up children the more they have come to the conclusion that what good mothers and fathers instinctively feel like doing for their babies is best after all." (*The Common Sense Book of Baby and Child Care*, chap. 1.)

But it's not that simple. As our neighbor has days she doesn't feel like getting into her garden, there are days even a good parent doesn't "instinctively" feel like coping with children.

But you pick a bouquet every day. And the rewards are great: "I have no greater joy than to hear that my children walk in truth." (3 Jn. 1:4.)

PARENTS, EASE THE PRESSURE

The young woman in the counselor's office had grown up in a luxurious home where both parents had been outstandingly successful. Now, off on her own, she realized she would never achieve such success or affluence. Her parents' expectations of her had been so unrealistic and now seemed so unattainable that at age twenty she had already branded herself a failure. She was being treated for severe depression.

As reported in the *New York Times*, hers was among cases discussed at a recent workshop in Connecticut examining the special pressures and difficulties faced by children of "fast-track parents."

Many such parents have become so blinded by their own ambitions, one psychotherapist reported, that they fail to see the effect their attitudes have on their children.

"These children see their mothers and fathers placing such priority on getting to the top that they worry that their parents won't love or respect them unless they do the same," she said.

"They must always have their eye on winning," another counselor said. "No wonder we see in them the diseases of adults, like ulcers and depression. Even minor personal shortcomings seem to trouble them more than others, because failure is so often met with condemnation rather than compassion."

Often, he added, such children underachieve because they

see the goal of meeting their parents' expectations as impossible.

Counselors urged parents to help a less competitive child develop a talent or skill that will provide an adequate income and a sense of pride, as well as a simpler, less pressured life. They argued that there is equal — if not greater — value in not seeking the highest-paying, most prestigious jobs, but work that, though lower in pay and status, provides a real public service.

This eminently sound advice is especially pertinent to LDS homes with our special understanding of the eternal destiny of the individual.

"Whatever principle of intelligence we attain unto in this life, it will rise with us in the resurrection. And if a person gains more knowledge and intelligence in this life through his diligence and obedience than another, he will have so much the advantage in the world to come." (D&C 130:18-19.)

That profound scripture makes the priorities clear. It speaks nothing of wealth or prestige. It speaks only of knowledge and intelligence, diligence and obedience. It makes no distinction between kinds of knowledge. Knowledge of high finance or corporate management is given no more weight in the eternal scheme of things than knowledge of how to build a beautiful cabinet or lay a lasting driveway.

What does count is doing whatever we do as well as we are capable of doing it. That and, as Jesus repeatedly emphasized, obedience and service.

Parents hungry and impatient for their children's status and wealth might well ponder how pointedly the Savior drove home that lesson. "And Jesus sat over against the treasury, and beheld how people cast money into the treasury: and many that were rich cast in much.

"And there came a certain poor widow, and she threw in two mites, which make a farthing.

"And he called unto him his disciples, and saith unto them,

Verily I say unto you, That this poor widow hath cast more in, than all they which have cast into the treasury.

"For all they did cast in of their abundance; but she of her want did cast in all that she had, even all her living." (Mark 12:41-44.)

If only parents could treat their children with such sensitivity and wisdom! If only they could understand and always remember that it is not the test score or the size of the salary check that counts, but the honesty and diligence of the effort.

Parents want their children to succeed. So does the Creator, but by a different, better, more eternal measure of success than many of us comprehend.

The wise parent will back off on the pressure and concentrate on helping the child understand and use the Savior's way of measuring.

LETTER TO A NEW TEENAGER

So today it happened. You became a teenager.

We've kidded you a lot about that. How all at once everything would change. How teenagers become so intolerant—and intolerable. How we hoped you'd still speak to us. How we hoped boys wouldn't become the only thing in your life. And on and on.

You knew it was all kidding, of course, and you put up with it patiently and with good humor. Patience and good humor have always been two of the lovable things about you.

Now let me tell you what I really think about your being a teenager.

First, how can it have happened so fast? It can't be thirteen years since your beautiful mother and proud father were showing off their firstborn and your grandparents were telling everyone who would listen about the most perfect grandchild ever born.

We've loved those thirteen years. Watching you develop through every phase of your babyhood and childhood has been pure joy.

We have loved your sensitivity and creativity that filled our souls and refrigerator doors with the beauty of, in turn, rainbows and hearts and stars and, now, flowers. We have marveled at how with each phase of your life you, yourself, have become more beautiful, inside and out.

We have no reason to doubt this process will continue, only in new and wondrous ways, as you cross the bridge from childhood to young womanhood.

But may a grandfather, with no other justification than that he loves you, offer some advice?

Don't cross the bridge too fast. Don't be impatient. To everything there's a season. Usually, the longer we delay a new experience, the more we appreciate and enjoy it. Wait for the right time. And when you have crossed the bridge, don't forget what was on the other side.

One endearing thing about your mother is that she has never lost the childlike qualities of loving fun, being teachable, losing herself in the wonder and excitement of new knowledge and new experience. You are in a remarkable and special way your mother's daughter; be like her in that.

With young womanhood come wondrous new urges. God put them there to help you form and preserve a loving, joyous, lasting relationship with the right man at the right time, and because He wants you as His partner in creating new life. Used in the way He intends, those urges can bring your greatest joy and fulfilment. Misused, they can bring tragedy.

There will be times, lots of them, when you will feel your parents are unfair or uncaring, that they don't understand, that they aren't with it or "cool." There will be times when they say no despite your pleas that the parents of every other teenager are saying yes.

These conflicts can't, apparently, be avoided. They are part of the territory as teenagers go about their important and proper task of asserting independence and learning to make their own decisions and parents go about theirs of nurturing and guiding and protecting.

At such times, can you remember just two things? First, that your parents have been over this road before. They know the blind curves. The road may change; the dangers don't. Second, your parents act the way they do because they love you — enough to risk your not, temporarily, liking them.

One more thing. Wherever you are, remember who you are—whose child, part of whose eternal family.

That's all the advice. You are smart enough and good enough and well enough taught that you need no more. When the tests come you will pass with honors because you will already have made the right decisions.

Have a great life. Your grandmother and grandfather love you more than you can possibly know until you have grandchildren of your own.

CHILDHOOD'S MINISTERING ANGELS

Hearts everywhere were touched by the story of Cecilia Cichan, lone survivor among 159 persons aboard the Northwest Airlines plane that crashed after takeoff from Detroit.

Cecilia, four, was found alive when rescuers heard faint whimperings in the wreckage. Her mother's body, shielding her in a last act of love, had saved her from the crash and the flames that followed.

As a social worker's letter in the *New York Times* points out, her rescue was a poignant reminder that life is filled with tragedy for many children and that emotional scars can be minimized only by constant infusions of love from relatives, friends, and professionals.

"However sad this case may be," the social worker writes, "it should also serve as a grim reminder that violent and sudden death, followed by the lifelong psychic pain resulting from such loss, confronts children every day in the United States. Not all of these young victims have two sets of grandparents, dozens of close relatives and friends, thousands of dollars in donations from strangers, and front-page news stories to look back on for solace. . . .

"I can no longer count how many little boys and girls I know who have survived crashes, witnessed the deaths of their parents by murder, accident or suicide, or been unwilling participants in violent family dramas that left them scarred and orphaned, in every possible way. . . . I see children who may be left with one elderly, sick grandparent, or with no grandparents and with no caring aunts and uncles, no front-page publicity, no outpouring of gifts, love, money or sympathy. . . . "

Add to this tragic list countless others who bear other kinds of trauma and misery—those with mental or physical disabilities, those with deep feelings of inadequacy or insecurity or guilt, those who feel alienated and lonely.

Without loving, nurturing support, these innocent children will grow up to become nonfunctional or antisocial adults. Society faces a heavy responsibility for these children. Meeting it will require far more effort than has been given.

But within the Church, not a single child need be without nurturing support, *if the system works as it should.* Consider the support team, in addition to the family, behind every child:

There are home teachers and visiting teachers, called to watch over the Church and qualified by the gift of discernment to do it.

There are Primary teachers and youth class and quorum advisers who, beyond simply teaching lessons, are responsible for each member. There are class and quorum officers to help meet that responsibility. There are presidencies to back them up.

There is a bishop whose major responsibility is the youth of the ward, and counselors to help.

There is the ward council whose most important item on the agenda should be to consider the individual needs of ward members.

There is the entire ward family as a resource for love and nurturing.

Never was the Savior's ministry of love more tenderly expressed than when He called a little child to Him and exhorted His followers: "And whoso shall receive one such little child in my name receiveth me . . . it is not the will of your Father which is in heaven, that one of these little ones should perish." (Matt. 18:5, 14.)

On another continent at another time, "... he took their little children, one by one, and blessed them, and prayed unto the Father for them.

"And when he had done this he wept again;

"And he spake unto the multitude, and said unto them: Behold your little ones.

" ... and they saw the heavens open, and they saw angels descending out of heaven as it were in the midst of fire; and they came down and encircled those little ones about, and they were encircled about with fire; and the angels did minister unto them." (3 Ne. 17:21-24.)

In His love for children, the Lord needs angels to minister here and now, today. Are we ready and willing?

HOW GRANDPARENTS SUCCEED

Because we learn more by example than by precept, funerals can be among the most instructive meetings we attend. Who can hear tributes paid to the life of one who dies strong in faith and beloved for service without taking new resolve to emulate that faith and service?

Every day funerals honor men and women who achieve no fame beyond their circle of family and friends, but who within that circle are heroes and heroines.

Such a man died recently. In his eighty-six years of life he achieved modest business success, gave faithful but not particularly noteworthy service in various Church callings, raised a reasonably successful but hardly famous family.

Nothing remarkable about that. What did stand out at his funeral was that this man had been a living textbook in how to be a successful grandfather.

His formula goes like this: First, there was his profound sense of the importance of family. His children and grandchildren learned at an early age they belonged to something special and important—a family that looked back to its roots with reverence and gratitude and forward to future generations with the greatest love and concern.

Not that he preached about family importance; he simply demonstrated it by the uncounted thousands of miles he traveled for the blessing of babies, baptisms, ordinations, graduations, weddings. No grandchild of his ever had cause to doubt his or her importance.

His determination to keep family ties strong led to family reunions every two years for over thirty years. Three- and four-day affairs they were, at mountain lakes, the seashore, the desert—always a new place. They followed his special formula—minimal business meetings and preaching, maximum togetherness, fun, and meaningful interchange.

"I want the grandchildren to come because they *want* to, not out of duty," he insisted. And come they did, year after year, from all over the country.

So the way he worked at building family love, unity, and importance was one part of his success formula. Coupled with it was his capacity to enjoy and be enjoyed.

On his eightieth birthday, the family prepared a book of his life, with a page from each grandchild describing "How I remember Grandpa." Many commented on his spiritual strength as patriarch of his family and a patriarch in the Church, of blessings given, private moments of counseling, his steadiness and reliability, the great, warm sense of love that surrounded him.

But many more—all, in fact—wrote of how much fun he was to be with, of his sense of humor, his love of games, the honor of being challenged by him to a game of Ping-Pong. They remembered sessions of Scrabble, carroms, "Stomp Your Neighbor." They remembered the nonsense songs he sang to them, the poems he recited, the magic tricks he performed. Almost all marveled at how he seemed to love life, how he never seemed to grow old.

If he had ever lectured on good grandparenting—and, of course, he never did—he would have said, "Enjoy your grandchildren. Play with them. Stay involved. Stay young. And always, always love them and let them know it."

One son who had departed somewhat from his father's faith spoke at the funeral, listing two other success qualities. First, he listed authority without severity. "I don't think any of us children ever questioned Father's authority," he said. "But it was never authority exercised by edict or threat. If we obeyed, it was because we respected the example of our father's life."

Second, he listed his father's unswerving devotion to his own faith, combined with complete empathy for those who did not share it. "Father was dogmatic (in the best sense of the word) in his devotion to his religious principles," he said. "At the same time, he was incapable of imposing judgment on those who did not share his vision. For me, this infinite capacity for unconditioned love made it possible to live a productive life with self-esteem.

"Unlike the biblical parent who was capable of welcoming the prodigal back into the fold, Father didn't even recognize the concept of a prodigal. A son was a son, and that was that."

Which was true, but it's also true that this man never left the slightest doubt in the minds of his children and grandchildren that his greatest hope, his constant, most fervent prayer, was that they share the faith and righteousness that would enable them to live with the family eternally.

Every child deserves a grandfather like that. What a tragedy, in this day of rootlessness and family fragmentation, that more don't have one.

THE PERILS OF PARENTING

Rearing children is a tough proposition these days. In most homes, the all-intrusive medium of television exposes children to harsh realities about as soon as — and in some cases sooner than — it does their parents.

Some parents are wise and strong and attentive enough to carefully limit their children's TV watching and minimize the damage. But that's not easy for overcommitted parents to accomplish. And even when they do, there's no way to insulate their children from those whose parents don't.

So successful parenting is hard — perhaps harder than it has ever been. But many families seem to manage it remarkably well. Can we learn from them any common denominators for success?

Volumes can be and have been written on techniques and strategies of parenting. But experience shows that what works for one set of parents may not for another. Only a few principles seem to apply universally. One is that a healthy self-image is essential if a child is to stand firm against the pressures of peers and the seductiveness of our TV-hyped society. It's the insecure youngster who hungers for acceptance who is most likely to get into drugs or illicit sex or other troubles.

So what are the essential elements in building a child's self-image? First and foremost, the child must be assured of the parents' unconditional love. That means love that does not depend on a child's achievements or meeting parents' expectations, that is not diminished if a child fails to measure up to the parents' desires. A child may quit trying to achieve rather than risk loss of parental love through failing.

Second, a child gets a powerful message of his self-worth when the parent cares enough to share feelings about their parent-child relationships. It's not easy; many parents never really verbalize these feelings. But without a genuine sharing of emotions, the child may not feel entirely secure about his place in his parents' hearts.

Third, it may help a child's self-esteem to learn, in appropriate times and ways, that the parents are not perfect. No child is perfect, and most are keenly, often painfully, aware of it. If a child can learn that parents are also striving to overcome weaknesses, it can do much to resolve self-doubt and give assurance of self-worth.

What assurance, for example, Helaman must have felt when he heard his father, Alma, describe the torment of his past: "I was racked with eternal torment, for my soul was harrowed up to the greatest degree and racked with all my sins. Yea, I did remember all my sins and iniquities, for which I was tormented with the pains of hell; yea, I saw that I had rebelled against my God, and that I had not kept his holy commandments." (Alma 36:12-13.)

Surely, Helaman must have felt, if his father could throw off such a past and become this great and holy leader who had accomplished so much good, he, too, had such potential.

How could he and his brother, Shiblon, doubt their importance in their father's eyes when he shared with them with such love the yearnings of his heart for their salvation? (See Alma 36-38.) And how could the third brother, Corianton, doubt his father's unconditional love, despite his sorrow for the son's sexual sins, when he gave to him one of scripture's great sermons on the gospel plan and a charge to go forth and preach the word? (See Alma 39-42.)

Alma's eloquence and spiritual strength were developed

by diligent effort after his earlier problems. They give us encouragement today to press forward and never give up. The principles he followed in building his sons' convictions of their self-worth are available to us all.

MESSAGES
FROM OUR
HERITAGE

A REBIRTH OF VISION

During the month of February, Americans pause to remember and honor two of the greatest men in their history—George Washington and Abraham Lincoln. But not only Americans should celebrate. If any American holiday ought to be given reverent attention by lovers of freedom everywhere, particularly by Latter-day Saints, it is Presidents' Day.

The nation founded, nurtured, and preserved by those two men has, through the years, been the exemplar of freedom, the standard to which men everywhere could aspire. More eternally important, in the soil of its freedom the restored gospel could be planted and grow; on the foundation of its economic strength the restored Church could be built worldwide.

It would be hard to imagine two men more disparate than these two who more than any others built the nation. Washington was the landed aristocrat, trained as an officer when soldiering was a gentleman's avocation, never an office-seeker, hardly eloquent with tongue or pen, stiff and formal with all but his intimate associates. Contrast Lincoln, the rail splitting, yarn spinning, rough-and-tumble wrestling, circuit-riding country lawyer, born in poverty and perpetually poor, repeatedly defeated as a politician, self-taught but a master of simple eloquence.

What did they have in common, these two? First and most

103

important, Latter-day Saints believe, they were raised up by God to meet the needs of their day. Washington did not speak much of spiritual things. Example spoke for him; the image of his kneeling in the snow that bitter winter at Valley Forge told his countrymen all they needed to know about the source of his strength. But in a prayer remarkably like Book of Mormon warnings that to prosper and remain free this nation must serve the God of the land, he pleaded:

"I make it my earnest prayer that God would have the United States in His Holy protection; that He would incline the hearts of the citizens to cultivate a spirit of subordination and obedience to government; to entertain a brotherly affection and love for one another. . . . And finally that He would dispose us all to do justice, to love mercy, and to demean ourselves with that charity, humility and pacific temper of mind which were the characteristics of the Divine Author of our blessed religion, and without an humble imitation of whose example in these things we can never hope to be a happy nation."

How badly such wisdom is needed today, when the doctrine of separation of church and state has been tortured to the point a federal judge has outlawed a team's prayer before a high school football game.

Lincoln was even more eloquent in his declaration of dependence on God. As he first left Illinois for the White House, his words of farewell concluded: "I now leave, not knowing when or whether I may return, with a task before me greater than that which rested upon Washington. Without the assistance of that Divine Being who ever attended him, I cannot succeed. With that assistance I cannot fail."

In the dark days when the fate of the Republic hung in the balance, he testified: "I am driven to my knees, because there is no place else to go."

And to a group of senators who came to argue with him about war and slavery, he uttered the same truth Washington and Book of Mormon prophets had earlier proclaimed:

"I not only believe that Providence is not unmindful of the

struggle in which this nation is engaged, that if we do not do right, God will let us go our own way to ruin; and that if we do right, He will lead us safely out of this wilderness, crown our armies with victory, and restore our dissevered Union . . . [in] accord with His plans of dealing with this Nation, in the midst of which He means to establish justice. I think He means that we shall do more than we have yet done in the furtherance of His plans and He will open the way for our doing it. I have felt His hand upon me in great trials, and submitted to His guidance, and I trust that as He shall farther open the way, I will be ready to walk therein, relying on His help and trusting in His goodness and wisdom."

These great men clearly saw the mission of America and the need for righteousness to fulfill it. How badly the nation today, as it flounders in its troubles at home and abroad, needs a rebirth of that kind of vision.

KEEPING THE REPUBLIC

The summer of 1787 in Philadelphia was unusually hot and humid. Despite the heat, and to preserve the confidentiality of what they were doing, the fifty-five men sweltering there kept the windows shut tight.

They labored under other difficulties besides heat. They came from twelve separate, diverse, and independent states. A thirteenth, Rhode Island, had refused to send a delegate. None of the states had empowered them to do what they were doing. They had been sent to Philadelphia to revise the Articles of Confederation, not to launch into a wholly unique experiment in government. The debates, dragging on for four months, were tense, often abrasive.

But finally they finished their work. A lady asked Benjamin Franklin what they had created. His reply: "A Republic, if you can keep it."

At the beginning of the third century of life under the Constitution of the United States, it is appropriate to ask: Can we? And how?

In the broad sense, the answer comes from the prophets of the Book of Mormon, who warned that this nation will remain free only as long as its people serve the God of the land, which is Jesus Christ. So the first bulwark to preserve the Republic is the righteousness of the people.

But there's a more specific obligation on citizens in preserving a government of the people. It is the obligation to participate fully and intelligently in the election process.

The exciting uniqueness of the Constitution created by those men at Philadelphia is that it is a grant of power by the people to a government which they — the people — had created. It is the *people's* government. The *people* have responsibility for it. There is profound wisdom in Franklin's response, that we'll have a Republic if *you* — the people, not the leaders — can keep it.

Throughout America, in the privacy and freedom of the voting booth, the people direct the government they have created. They elect the senators and representatives who determine the character of Congress for the next two years. They elect the governors and the legislators who will make the laws in all fifty states. They elect the officials who will govern every county in the nation, and the school boards that will shape the country's educational system. In short, the voters determine the kind of country we will have.

Modern scripture leaves no doubt about the responsibility of citizens to cast not a blind but an informed vote in elections at every level of government. Section 104 of the Doctrine and Covenants clearly states our obligations. It has been accepted by the Church as scripture, and is as binding as any other scripture. It states:

God holds men accountable for making laws and administering them for the good of society.

The people should seek out and uphold civil officers and magistrates who will administer the law in equity and justice.

All men are bound to sustain and uphold the government as long as it upholds their inherent and inalienable rights.

How does one sustain and uphold our government? By loving it and valuing it as a priceless gift of God through inspired men. By holding fast to the principles on which it was founded. But more than that. To really sustain government, one must be actively involved in it, raising one's voice and casting one's vote to correct its faults, to choose able and righteous representatives, and to direct their actions.

All that is necessary for the triumph of evil, it has been wisely said, is for good men to do nothing. If good men and women do little or nothing to influence the electoral process, evil will certainly triumph in this nation.

The Latter-day Saint who fails to become informed on issues and candidates during the election season and fails to cast an informed vote fails not only the responsibilities of citizenship but also the responsibilities of membership in God's kingdom.

FOR THE PURSUIT OF HAPPINESS

*We hold these truths to be self-evident, that all
men are created equal, that they are endowed
by their Creator with certain unalienable
Rights, that among these are Life, Liberty, and
the pursuit of Happiness.*

With those words and the remarkable document that followed, a nation was born. But the Declaration of Independence was more than the birth pronouncement of a nation.
It was a bold affirmation of concepts inborn in man from the
beginning. It was a clarion signal that concepts smothered or
ignored during most of mankind's time on earth were now,
at last, to be the guiding principles of a new society.

They were — and are — more than a justification of America's
struggle for independence. They were — and are — a message
of hope for mankind everywhere.

The truths that men are born equal, that they possess certain
unalienable rights, that governments exist by the consent of
the governed were of ancient origin. But they had never before
been tried in actual practice. It was the boldest of experiments
the fifty-six signers of the Declaration of Independence were
undertaking.

They were not irresponsible radicals, those fifty-six.
Twenty-four were lawyers and jurists. Eleven were merchants.

Nine were farmers and large plantation owners. They were men of means, educated, secure. They well understood the consequences of their act, and many of them suffered grievous consequences. Their homes and properties were looted and destroyed, businesses lost, families scattered. Many died in poverty, broken in body if not in spirit.

Why? What would light such fires in the bellies of such men? They were a disparate lot. They were English, Irish, Scottish, and Welsh. They were Germans, Dutch, Swedes, French. They or their ancestors had come to this land for many reasons — some to escape religious persecution, some for adventure, some for economic opportunity, some simply to get out of prison.

But they had a common bond. They worshipped a Savior who was born to bring truth into the world and had taught that with truth comes freedom. They shared an Old Testament whose prophets proclaimed liberty. They knew that God created man to be free.

Knowledge like that gives men courage to do incredible things.

Around the Fourth of July, we speak much of liberty. But there were two other unalienable rights emphasized in the Declaration of Independence — life and the pursuit of happiness. The right to life is fundamental, of course — though, tragically, it has all too often been ignored by the terrorists of the world, today as well as anciently.

What of the right to the pursuit of happiness? No political document had ever before expressed that as an explicit right for its citizens. But it was a commonplace concept of the eighteenth century that God and natural law intended that men should be happy. Rousseau wrote that happiness is "the first desire impressed on us by nature, and the only one that never leaves us." Voltaire declared that "Happiness is the object, the duty, and the goal of all sensible men." Adam Smith taught that "the purpose of governments is to promote the happiness of those who live under them."

Book of Mormon scripture is more all-encompassing and more explicit. "Men are, that they might have joy," Lehi simply and directly taught his son Jacob in that remarkable sermon on the plan of salvation.

So they were right on target, those men who pledged their lives, their fortunes, and their sacred honor in signing that declaration. Their message speaks not only to Americans but to all people. Life, liberty, the pursuit of happiness are — or should be — universal rights.

Universal, too, is the prescription for preserving those rights, regardless of where a man lives or the political system under which he is governed. The Lord has made it explicitly clear as far as America is concerned: Liberty, security, prosperity can be ours only as long as we serve the God of the land, Jesus Christ. Certainly other nations can hope for these blessings only on the same terms.

As for happiness, Joseph Smith summarized what the Lord has told us through the centuries: "Happiness is the object and design of our existence and will be the end thereof *if* we pursue the path that leads to it; and this path is virtue, uprightness, faithfulness, holiness, and keeping all the commandments of God."

THE WISDOM OF THE MASS

In all the rich legacy of gospel scholarship and teaching left by President Marion G. Romney in his lifetime of service, a statement he made in general conference several years ago rings with special meaning and authority:

"The truth I desire to emphasize today is that mortals are in very deed the literal offspring of God. If men understood, believed, and accepted this truth, our sick and dying society would be reformed and redeemed.

"Members of The Church of Jesus Christ of Latter-day Saints accept this concept as a basic doctrine of their theology. The lives of those who have given it thought enough to realize its implications are controlled by it; it gives meaning and direction to all their thoughts and deeds.

"The aspirations, desires, and motivations of one who accepts, believes, and by the power of the Holy Spirit obtains a witness to the truth that he is a begotten son or daughter unto God differs from the aspirations of him who believes otherwise, as the growing vine differs from the severed branch." (Conference Report, April 1973.)

That conviction has been the source of much of the progress of mankind. From it stems the belief that man is perfectible, that he is capable of governing himself, that, indeed, he was endowed by his Creator with certain unalienable rights, including life, liberty, and the pursuit of happiness.

That is the underlying belief that led such men as Thomas Jefferson and James Madison to build a solid foundation for America's inspired system of self-government, drawing on the work of men like John Locke and Thomas Hobbes and on a gradually developing political philosophy reaching clear back to the Magna Carta.

But even that wasn't the beginning. More than two thousand years ago, another remarkable political philosopher laid out for his people a system of government based on the same principles. His name was Mosiah, the latest in a long succession of kings—some righteous, many not—that had ruled in the land we now call the Americas:

The time for kings was past, he argued. "Behold, I say unto you, the sins of many people have been caused by the iniquities of their kings; therefore their iniquities are answered upon the heads of their kings. And now I desire that this inequality should be no more in this land, especially among this my people; but I desire that this land be a land of liberty, and every man may enjoy his rights and privileges alike. . . . " (Mosiah 29:31-32.)

To accomplish it, he established a government in which the "burden should come upon all the people, that every man might bear his part." (Mosiah 29:34.) Judges were to be elected by the voice of the people. The people were to be free, but they were also to be responsible.

That kind of government rests on faith in man's basic nature. In establishing the first known system of self-government on the American continent, Mosiah expressed that faith: "Now it is not common that the voice of the people desireth anything contrary to that which is right; but it is common for the lesser part of the people to desire that which is not right; therefore this shall ye observe and make it your law—to do your business by the voice of the people." (Mosiah 29:26.)

Two thousand years later, another inspired political philosopher, President J. Reuben Clark, expressed the same conviction in similarly strong terms: "I have complete confidence in the aggregate wisdom of the . . . people, if they are given and made to understand the facts.

"The wisdom of the mass is always greater than the wisdom of the individual or of the group. The few may be more subtle, more agile-minded, more resourceful; they may for a time push to the front and scamper ahead in the march; they may on occasion and for a time entice us down the wrong highway at the crossroads.

"But the great slow-moving deliberate-thinking mass plods along over the years down the Divinely appointed way. Led astray, they slowly, cumberously swing back to the right road, no matter what the toil or the sacrifice may be, and when they start the return, they crush whatever lies in their path. So has humanity come up through the ages." (Cited in Book of Mormon [Religion 121-122] student manual, pp. 209-10.)

The aggregate wisdom of the people can be trusted because the people have within them the seeds of Godhood. They can follow wrong paths for long periods of time, even, as the Nephites did, to destruction. But no one who believes President Romney's testimony of the divine origin of man can doubt his capacity to govern himself as God intended.

WE OWE IT TO OUR COMMUNITY

It was swearing-in day for the new town council. After a spirited campaign, a new mayor had been elected and two new councilmen — or, in this case, councilwomen. One was a Latter-day Saint, the first elected to office in years in this resort town where Church influence had been remarkably small. A mother of four, Primary worker, piano teacher, author, Cub Scout leader, and local school volunteer, she certainly needed nothing more to do, but had yielded to pleas that "One of us ought to get into this race; why not you?"

The oaths were taken. The new mayor popped a bottle of champagne and filled glasses of council members for a toast to the town. When he came to the new councilwoman's glass, he stopped, turned to the crowd, and good-naturedly announced: "One abstention."

There had been no flaunting of Church membership during the campaign, nor is there likely to be during coming years of service on the council. Only quiet holding to principles, genuine friendship and respect for people of all beliefs, a commitment to work together to make the town a better place to live. Enormous influence for good can come from that kind of effective involvement in community affairs.

It's not always easy for active Church members to involve themselves in community service. Pressures on time and energy are already great. Family commitments take precedence —

and should. Church activities and the circle of Church associates can so satisfy social needs that there is little incentive or stimulus to be involved elsewhere.

But Church leaders don't encourage insularity. They have always urged constructive, helpful involvement in community affairs. One of the reasons given for the consolidated meeting schedule was to free more time for community service.

Why is such service important? For at least three reasons: First, it is something we *ought* to do. Service, someone has said, is the rent we pay for the space we occupy on earth. That space isn't confined to the ward house. It includes the communities that guard our lives and property, that clean our streets and carry away our garbage and mow our parks. It includes the schools our children attend. It includes dozens of volunteer organizations that serve the needy or improve public health or provide cultural or recreational opportunities that enrich our lives.

These organizations don't go by themselves. People make them go. Isn't making them go part, at least, of what the Lord intended when He told us: "Men [and women] should be anxiously engaged in a good cause, and do many things of their own free will, and bring to pass much righteousness"? (D&C 58:27.)

Second, this is a time when the involvement and influence of straight-thinking, morally sound people is needed in public affairs as perhaps never before. Standards and morality are under siege at all levels of society. Church members need to remember the truth of Edmund Burke's statement: "The only thing necessary for the triumph of evil is for good men to do nothing."

Third, we can only influence those lives that we touch. Touching lives means getting involved with them, and there is no better way than working together for a common good. Community service is an excellent way to achieve what Edwin Markham described so memorably in his poem, "Outwitted":

116

He drew a circle that shut me out—
Heretic, rebel, a thing to flout.
But Love and I had the wit to win:
We drew a circle that took him in.

Of course, it's important to keep priorities straight. Family and church come first. Personal lives need to be kept in balance. Community service must not be allowed to come between husband and wife, parent and child. Nor must it be allowed to interfere with fundamentals like scripture study, temple attendance, individual compassionate service.

But with planning and organization, with cooperative participation by the entire family, with willingness to give up a few nonessentials—a few television shows a week, for example—most of us can find the time to enrich ourselves, improve our moral, physical, and social environment, and fulfill our citizenship obligations through community service.

OUR ELECTION-YEAR CHALLENGES

Once the noise and posturing of the two national party conventions are out of the way, Americans settle in to the serious task of electing their national, as well as state and local, leaders.

It can be a confusing task. Television makes personality and image more important than character or issues. In their zeal to be elected, candidates don't always stick to the truth or to the highest ethical standards. The candidate's past life comes under the magnifying glass. Personal attacks, exaggerated if not manufactured, are seized upon and blown up by sensation-seeking media. Given the nature of our election process, it's a wonder that good men and women can still be found to seek elective office.

In the heat and confusion of election time, it is important to keep certain principles in mind.

One is the Church's political impartiality. The First Presidency has repeatedly emphasized that it endorses no party or candidate. With that emphasis comes the caution, also, that no Church facility or meeting should be used for political purposes.

Another principle is that Latter-day Saints have a special responsibility to cut through the demagoguery of the election campaign to the real issues. They have been taught that God holds men accountable both for making laws and administering

118

them, for the good and safety of society. (See D&C 134:1.) That surely means we are responsible to learn the issues and to make every effort to identify and elect the candidates with the right stands on those issues.

Finally, the Lord expects us to cast our votes on the basis of character rather than television glibness or catchy billboards. He exhorted us that officials who "will administer the law in equity and justice should be sought for and upheld by the voice of the people." (D&C 134:3.)

Sought for. That's an active verb that requires active participation in the political process. It takes effort. It allows no tolerance for the passivity that sends so many voters to the polls — if they go at all — ignorant and unprepared.

The perils of passivity are nowhere more dramatically illustrated than among the Book of Mormon peoples at the time of Nephi, the son of Helaman. Evil men had taken over the republic Mosiah had established, "having usurped the power and authority of the land; laying aside the commandments of God . . . doing no justice unto the children of men; condemning the righteous because of their righteousness; letting the guilty and the wicked go unpunished because of their money. . . . " (Hel. 7:4-5.)

Men like that have, from time to time, infiltrated government in our day. But not many, nor have they stayed long in office. America's tradition of responsible government is strong, and in the main its office-holders have been, and are, honorable men and women. That is one of this country's greatest blessings, and the strongest surety of its freedom.

But, as Book of Mormon prophets as well as latter-day statesmen have emphasized, there's nothing automatic about keeping that blessing. Two hundred years ago, the patriot John Philpot Curran sounded a warning as appropriate today as it was in 1790: "It is the common fate of the indolent to see their rights become a prey to the active. The condition upon which God hath given liberty to man is eternal vigilance."

119

Someone has traced the rise and fall of nations in eight steps:
- From bondage to spiritual faith.
- From spiritual faith to courage.
- From courage to freedom.
- From freedom to abundance.
- From abundance to selfishness.
- From selfishness to complacency.
- From complacency to apathy.
- From apathy back again into bondage.

On that continuum, America stands somewhere between selfishness and complacency, or maybe a bit beyond. Will we continue on to the next step, and the next? Heaven forbid; but can we muster the political energy and vigilance to prevent it?

WILL WE FLINCH AT THE WORK?

Four days after the Mormon pioneers arrived in Salt Lake Valley, Brigham Young stood near the right fork of City Creek, planted his cane, and declared: "Here we will build the Temple of our God." That was before the new city was laid out, before planting was completed, before homes were begun. President Young left no doubt where his priorities lay.

The struggle to secure a foothold in the new desert valley home was so demanding it took six years before work started on the temple. But start it did. While the builders were still living in log cabins and fighting crickets, they set out to build the most massive, lasting, inspiring edifice they could conceive. They did it with little money and with the nearest supply of metal and tools a thousand miles away.

As the work began, April 6, 1853, President Young spoke: "I do not like to prophesy much. . . . But I will venture to guess that this day, and the work we have performed on it, will be long remembered by this people, and be sounded as with a trumpet's voice throughout the world." Brave words from a people still struggling for survival in a remote desert valley.

The foundation required a trench twenty feet deep, sixteen feet wide. Digging it took nine thousand man-days of labor. Some must have grumbled that, "We don't need a temple this big." But they kept digging.

The foundation was hardly finished when a federal army

threatened invasion to put down a supposed Mormon revolt. President Young made plans to evacuate the city, burn it to the ground if necessary. He ordered the temple excavation filled in, the foundation covered, the land leveled to appear as a newly plowed field.

When the threat of war passed, they dug it out again and started on the walls. They could have used sandstone; there was plenty nearby and it was easy to work with. But this structure was to last forever. So they went twenty miles away to Little Cottonwood Canyon to cut massive blocks of granite.

At first, with great labor, they dug a canal to float the blocks to the temple site. But this didn't work well, so all during the 1860s and 1870s, four- and six-oxen teams could be seen dragging the huge granite blocks those twenty miles.

Each stone had be cut to a precise size and shape. Sharpening the chisels was a never-ending job. Even with immense labor, it took nearly three years to cut and lay the six hundred stones needed for just one level.

Twenty years after the work began, the walls were barely visible above ground. But the prophet encouraged: "The Temple will be built as soon as we are prepared to use it." Meanwhile, so inspired was his vision and strong his faith that he began the building of temples in St. George, Manti, and Logan—all of them finished before the Salt Lake Temple was completed.

"Can you accomplish the work, you Latter-day Saints?" President Young challenged. "Have you the necessary faith; have you sufficient of the Spirit of God in your hearts to say, yes, by the help of God our Father we will erect these buildings to his name?"

The answer was unequivocal. They did, and forty long, hard years after it began, the work was finished. As he laid the capstone, April 6, 1892, President Wilford Woodruff declared: "If there is any scene on the face of this earth that will attract the attention of the God of Heaven and the heavenly host, it is the one before us today—the assembling of this people, the shout of 'Hosanna,' the laying of the topstone of this temple in honor to our God."

But at that point, great and heroic as their work had been, the labor of temple-building was only well begun. In the ninety-five years since that stirring event, thirty-six temples have been built and dedicated. Several more are under construction. Soon, the work of eternal salvation will be going forward within the walls of forty-one temples in twenty-three different lands.

Building temples in places so far from Temple Square gives real meaning to the concept of a worldwide Church. It means people can stay and build up the Church where they live, and enjoy the fullest blessings of the gospel. It means newly called missionaries can go to missionary training centers near their homes; twelve such centers have been established in areas where temples exist.

So the work goes on, at an accelerating pace, nearly a century after the great temple in Salt Lake City was completed. Few are called to sacrifice as its builders did, but the call is the same — to qualify ourselves for eternal life through the temple ordinances and to seek out and qualify our ancestors in the same way.

The builders of the Salt Lake Temple, and so many others, never flinched in the face of their awesome task. Will we?

WHY PIONEERS SUCCEED

Most Church members know that on a hot July day in 1847, the Mormon pioneers first entered Salt Lake Valley. Most pause on or around July 24 to honor their faith and courage. But few know just *how* the pioneers entered the valley. Even fewer realize that the manner of their entering illustrates the difference between successful pioneering and failure.

The Mormons weren't the first pioneers in Salt Lake Valley. A year earlier came the ill-starred Donner party. Beguiled into taking an untried new shortcut to California, the party had left the known trail at Fort Bridger in what is now Wyoming. They struggled and bickered their way down Echo Canyon, over Big and Little Mountains, down Emigration Canyon almost to its mouth — and stopped. The canyon narrowed and deepened at that point. Choked with brush and boulders, it seemed impassable.

Characteristically, they didn't try. Three times before, facing what they knew would be a difficult passage, they had turned aside into the easier-seeming unknown. Each time got them into deeper trouble. Here, they did it again. Instead of hacking their way through the narrow gorge, they chose to climb a hill that rose so steeply from the canyon floor they had to hitch almost every yoke of oxen to each of their twenty-three wagons.

Twenty-three times those beasts climbed Donner Hill that day before the party finally entered Salt Lake Valley. Worn out, the animals needed rest. But there was no time; the season was far too late. On the party pushed, into the waterless wastes of the west Utah salt flats. Played out, the oxen couldn't make it. Unhitched and driven ahead to find water, many stampeded and were lost. Precious days were spent looking for them. Disorganized now and dangerously late, the party straggled on to the Sierra Nevada mountains where early snowstorms caught them just short of the summit. Only forty-seven of the eighty-two emigrants survived the dreadful winter that followed.

A year later, Brigham Young's Mormon pioneer company, following the Donner tracks, reached the gorge below Donner Hill. They, too, acted characteristically. Two men were sent to explore up the hill, down the other side, then back through the brushy gorge. They reported, as William Clayton's journal records, that: "A good road can soon be made down the canyon by digging a little and cutting through the bushes some ten or fifteen rods."

That was all they needed to know. Clayton's journal continues: "A number of men went to work immediately to make the road. . . . After spending four hours' labor the brethren succeeded in cutting a pretty good road along the creek and the wagons proceeded on. . . ."

The beauty and prosperity of Salt Lake Valley today, the strength and worldwide outreach of the Church that has grown from what they brought to the valley that July day, testify that the men driving those wagons were men committed to success.

But what makes success? What does Donner Hill tell of the difference between successful pioneering and failure? Success requires leaders with the wisdom and foresight to find out what lies ahead. It demands the faith and discipline to follow such leaders. It takes willing, effective cooperation; there's profound meaning in Clayton's words, "A number of men went to work immediately to make the road. . . ."

And it takes a sense of mission; those men knew why they had traveled a thousand miles of wilderness and why they were

125

making that road. They were establishing Zion. They were building the kingdom of God.

But that work is not finished. Carrying it forward from that day in 1847 to the Church's present strength and scope has taken the same pioneering qualities, in many lands and times. We see them reflected in the dedication of temples in Europe, Asia, Latin America, and elsewhere. We see them in the calling and labor of over 30,000 missionaries in the field. We see them in the faithful, selfless service of men and women at all levels of Church leadership and teaching.

And with all that, the greatest challenges still lie ahead. The higher the Church's profile becomes, the greater its size and strength, the more intense will be the opposition. Moving steadily forward in the face of that opposition will require the same qualities that took the pioneers around Donner Hill.

YOKE SACRIFICE WITH WISDOM

Sacrifice, the Latter-day Saint hymn tells us, brings forth the blessings of heaven. It is, moreover, the lifeblood of the Church, now as from the beginning. Without leaders and members who willingly give of themselves, there is no progress.

But to be effective in building the kingdom, sacrifice needs direction. Given in wisdom and in harmony with counsel, it can accomplish wonders. Given otherwise, it can bring tragedy. For example:

Winter came early and with bitter fury on the high plains of Wyoming in 1856. It caught more than one thousand faithful, struggling, sacrificing Latter-day Saints unprepared. In the next few weeks, starvation and cold snuffed out the lives of some 210 of them, with many others to die later of exposure. These were members of the Willie and Martin handcart companies, whose ordeal is one of the most tragic, heroic events in the history of western pioneering.

Almost from the arrival of the Mormon pioneers in Salt Lake Valley in 1847, Church leaders had appealed to members to gather to build the new land. To assist those unable to meet the costs of emigration, Brigham Young established a revolving fund, loans from which were to be repaid after roots were established in the new land. The flood of emigrants grew and reached a peak in 1855 — just as a drought and plague of grasshoppers left Zion in economic distress.

With the Perpetual Emigration Fund depleted and thousands seeking to come, Brigham Young proposed a solution: "We cannot purchase wagons and teams as in years past," he wrote. "I am consequently thrown back on my old plan—to make handcarts and let the emigration foot it.... They can come just as quick, if not quicker, and much cheaper—can start earlier and escape the prevailing sickness which annually lays so many of our brethren in the dust."

With characteristic Mormon efficiency, the program was launched. Church agents in England arranged ship passage. Others in Iowa City, Iowa, arranged to build the handcarts and organize and outfit the emigrants. Three handcart companies with a total of 815 men, women, and children left Iowa City by mid-June, 1856, and reached the valley in good shape by October 2.

Ironically, and tragically, the two largest handcart companies were the ones struck by disaster. Delayed in sailing and again in outfitting, the company led by returning missionary James G. Willie did not leave Iowa City until July 15. The Edward Martin Company left thirteen days later. Both companies were warned that the season was far too late and they faced grave risks. But enthusiasm for the gathering was high; the vote was taken to proceed, with faith that the weather would be tempered.

It wasn't. The first winter storm, much earlier than usual, hit on October 19, just as the Martin Company had become thoroughly soaked in the last crossing of the Platte River near present-day Casper, Wyoming. Deaths started almost immediately and mounted daily in both companies as blizzards swept the plains, and temperatures plummeted far below zero. Starving and exhausted, the two companies could only huddle in their bitter camps, praying for rescue.

The rescue effort was prompt and efficient. On October 4 Brigham Young learned the handcart companies were still on the Wyoming plains. The next day in October conference, his sermon was brief and to the point.

"Many of our brethren and sisters are on the plains with handcarts and we must send assistance to them. . . . That is my religion; that is the dictation of the Holy Ghost that I possess. It is to save the people. . . . I will tell you all that your faith, religion, and profession of religion, will never save one soul of you in the Celestial Kingdom of God, unless you carry out just such principles as I am now teaching you. *Go and bring in those people now on the plains.*"

In two days the first sixteen four-mule teams were on the way; by the end of October, 250 relief wagons. By early November the rescuers had the survivors moving again, but the ordeal was not ended. At the Sweetwater River, for example, three eighteen-year-old boys in the rescue company carried nearly every member of the Martin company across, suffering such exposure that all three soon died.

The tragedy of the Willie and Martin companies has branded the entire handcart program a failure. It wasn't. Eight other companies crossed the plains between 1856 and 1860, bringing 1,886 persons ranging from infants to aged men and women. In those companies, forty to forty-five persons died en route, a remarkably small number given the hardships of the journey.

Those who made it — and those who did not — live in memory as inspiring examples of courage, dedication, and sacrifice. It's a memory, as well as a lesson, that should never die.

A DAY FOR REMEMBERING

"This 30th of May, 1868, is designated for the purpose of strewing with flowers, or otherwise decorating the graves of comrades who died in defense of their country during the late rebellion, — and whose bodies now lie in almost every city, village and hamlet churchyard in the land.

"We should guard their graves with sacred vigilance. All that the consecrated wealth and taste of the nation can add to their adornment and security is but a fitting tribute to the memory of her slain defenders.... Let no neglect, no ravage of time, testify to the present or to the coming generations that we have forgotten as a people the cost of a free and undivided republic.

"If other eyes grow dull and other hands slack, and other hearts cold in the solemn trust, ours shall keep it well and long as the light and warmth of life remain in us."

With those words of Major General John A. Logan, Memorial Day became part of American life. In the years since then it has evolved into much more than a remembrance of Civil War dead. It is a time to remember and honor those who in all wars, declared and undeclared, have given the ultimate sacrifice in defense of country. Nor is such honor due only from and for Americans; people of every nation owe a debt of gratitude for those who died fighting on their behalf.

Memorial Day is still more than this. It is a time also for

remembering and strengthening family bonds. The act of placing flowers on the grave of a long-gone ancestor—or a departed companion or child or any family member—is an expression of gratitude for all that person has meant in our lives. It is also recognition that family ties are, or should be, eternal.

Decorating graves is an appropriate and beautiful way of keeping fresh and bright that sense of the eternal, that sense of connection of the present to the past and to the future. An even better way is to live, here and now, for the eternal—keeping strong the ties of the living family, living worthy of the hopes and prayers of those who have gone before, teaching saving principles to those who will come after.

For Latter-day Saints, the day can and should be yet more. As we honor those heroes who died in uniform to build or preserve earthly kingdoms, should we not honor as well those heroes who gave so much to build the Kingdom of God?

Who are they? The Prophet Joseph, of course, and that small group of courageous men and women who faced ridicule and mobbings and death to give life to the infant kingdom. And, of course, the pioneers who made that historic trek to reestablish it in the Western wilderness.

But more than these. Pioneering did not end with Brigham Young. Should we not remember and honor on this day those countless other pioneers, those who went on beyond the valley of the Great Salt Lake, answering calls to settle isolated mountain valleys and arid deserts, facing floods and droughts, hunger and despair, to extend the stakes of the Church?

And what of all the others, through the many years, who have built the kingdom and made our lives what they are today? The missionaries who gave years of their lives to bring the gospel to us or our ancestors. The bishops whose devotion and love were so unfailing. The teachers. The quorum leaders. The Relief Society sisters. So many people have done so much.

Memorial Day is for remembering—and for giving thanks. How much we owe of both.

MESSAGES
OF LOVE

TOUCHING THE LEPER

*And there came a leper to him, beseeching
him, and kneeling down to him, and saying
unto him, If thou wilt, thou canst make me
clean.
And Jesus, moved with compassion, put
forth his hand, and touched him, and saith
unto him, I will; be thou clean.
And as soon as he had spoken, immediately
the leprosy departed from him, and he was
cleansed. (Mark 1:40-42.)*

That event seems simple, even commonplace, compared to
such dramatic miracles as raising the dead. But it reflects as
well, perhaps, as anything He did the central message of the
Savior's ministry.

It is hard for us today to imagine the awful condition of
the leper in New Testament times. He was considered legally
dead. But, worse, he was considered morally unclean. Forbid-
den to enter any walled city—lashed thirty-nine times if he
did—he wandered, muffled to the eyes, crying "Unclean!"

Under Jewish law, no one could greet him. Under the law,
no one could approach within six feet of the leper—one
hundred feet if the wind came from his direction. Any building
he entered was considered defiled and had to be purified. The

135

common practice was to throw stones at or run and hide from any leper who approached.

Such was the man who came to Jesus. What compassion and greatness he must have sensed in the Master to break the law in this manner. And what was the response? Against all law and tradition, Jesus reached out and touched the leper and by His touch cleansed him of his filthiness. By His touch, to save His brother, Jesus descended lower than any man—exactly as He did, later, to save each of us.

We are that leper, each of us unclean in his own way, each of us crying, "If thou wilt, thou canst make me clean." Each of us trusts that because of His infinite love, we will receive His touch.

And what does He ask in return? These words sum it up: Love one another even as I have loved you.

How can we? We have no divine power to redeem as He did. But what we can do is *touch* each other. There are lepers among us. They may be the people next door in the throes of a devastating divorce, or the teenager down the block trapped by drugs. It may be a friend's daughter facing forced marriage, or the fellow-quorum member who has lost his testimony. It may be the bleary-eyed man huddled outside the transient shelter waiting for the soup kitchen to open. It may be any unhappy, despondent, guilt-ridden human being who feels physically or morally unclean.

If we love as the Savior loved, we will reach out and touch—and heal. It really happens. In a prosperous LDS ward, the son of one of the most respected members got caught up in the drug culture. It led him into sin and eventually into crime.

Visiting him in jail, his bishop found him in despair, deeply penitent, longing to come back. "But Bishop, how can I?" he cried. "I have disgraced my parents and betrayed everyone who loved me. I can't associate with decent people again."

With a silent prayer, the bishop responded: "You come back to the ward. Don't dwell on what you have done. Forget it and let everyone else forget it. I promise you the people of the ward will put their arms around you and love you so you will never get away again."

The challenge was accepted, and the ward members justified the bishop's faith in them. They reached out and touched him. And, miraculous as it seems, the healing was complete.

The Lord has showered us with blessings beyond counting—life on this glorious earth, the loved ones with whom He has surrounded us, the peace and plenty we enjoy, the redeeming sacrifice that gives these and all other blessings eternal meaning. He asks so little in return. But the one thing He asks more urgently and repeatedly than any other is simple and unmistakable: That we love one another.

We can give nothing greater in gratitude for His greatest of all gifts to us than to follow Him in touching the leper.

SEEK THE LIVING WATER

Headlines in the daily press tell a woeful story of suffering caused by the barriers of race, religion, nationalism, and political philosophy men have erected against each other.

Terrorists kidnap and hijack and bomb, to the point tourists fear to travel in many parts of the world. In the Mideast, and spilling over into bloodshed elsewhere, it's Jew against Muslim, Muslim against Christian, Sunni Muslim against Shiite Muslim, moderate against fundamentalist. In Ireland, it's Catholic against Protestant, Irish against British. In South Africa, it's white against black, black radical against black moderate. In India, it's Sikh against Brahmin. In Nicaragua, it's Communist against Contra, mirroring the struggle raging in so many other parts of the world. And, brooding over it all, it's superpower against superpower, each with nuclear capacity to destroy the world as we know it.

Is there no remedy, no way men can live in security, free of fear? Is there no way to bridge the chasms of suspicion and fear and hatred?

There is a way. At a well in a much-scorned part of Palestine, He whose example we are invited to follow showed the way. Worn and thirsting after a long walk from Judea, Jesus came to the well in Samaria dug by Jacob centuries earlier. Of a Samaritan woman come to draw water he asked for a drink.

In a land where water is life, such a request was never

138

refused. But her answer came with obvious surprise: "How is it that thou, being a Jew, askest drink of me, which am a woman of Samaria? for the Jews have no dealings with the Samaritans." (John 4:9.)

How natural it would have been for others to turn from such a one in disgust. She was a woman; Jews of that age had no more conversation with women than necessary. She was a sinner, a woman who, having had five husbands, was now living with a man not her husband; Levitical law makes deadly clear how Jewish society regarded that.

Most damning, she was a Samaritan. Today, it's hard to comprehend what that meant. Alfred Edersheim, the nineteenth century Jewish/Christian scholar, in his excellent book *Life and Times of Jesus*, describes the Samaritan condition:

Samaria, the area between Judea and Galilee, was inhabited by foreigners after Israel was taken captive. When the Jews returned from captivity in Babylon, they refused to have anything to do with the idolatrous racial mixture in Samaria. Centuries of bitterness followed.

The Samaritans built a rival temple, repudiating all connection with Israel and dedicating their temple to Jupiter. While the Jews agonized under the Roman heel, the Samaritans prospered, even selling many Jews into slavery and waylaying and killing Jewish pilgrims on their way to Jerusalem.

The Jews retaliated, Edersheim recounts, by treating the Samaritans with every mark of contempt, accusing them of falsehood and irreligion, disowning them as to race or religion. To the Jews, Shechem, the Samaritan capital, was "the city of fools, derided by all men." To partake of Samaritan bread was like eating the flesh of swine.

Heir to this bitter history, Jesus faced the woman who had scorned Him. Forgetting His thirst, ignoring centuries of hatred and mistrust, He taught and loved.

He did not temporize: "Ye worship ye know not what," He told her. "We know what we worship: for salvation is of the Jews." (John 4:22.)

But who was right, or wrong, was to Him far less important than to teach that wherever God is worshipped, He is to be worshipped in spirit and truth.

So to this common, ignorant, sinful Samaritan woman, of all people, He for the first time revealed Himself, in plainness, to be the promised Messiah. With her and her people he spent two days, seeking to give to them the living water that springs up into eternal life. And many of these despised people believed and recorded their plain and simple testimony that this was the Christ, the Savior of the world.

Can nations and races and individuals not learn from that divine example: That while we properly hold to convictions of who and what is right, there is a higher truth. It is that we are all brothers, that God loves us all. We are more alike in our longing for peace and safety and dignity than we are different.

Jesus' treatment of the despised Samaritans with love and compassion opened the way for a rich harvest of souls who joined His followers in brotherhood in later years. Can we not follow Him?

WHOSE NEIGHBOR AM I?

As was so often the case during His ministry, it was a sticky situation Jesus faced. His teachings of a new gospel had deeply disturbed tradition-bound Jewish leaders. Enemies surrounded Him. Some had tried to kill Him. Again and again, others had tried to trap Him with His own words.

Now, as recorded in the tenth chapter of Luke, here was this lawyer testing Him, publicly asking the most fundamental of all questions: "What shall I do to inherit eternal life?"

The answer should have been obvious to any Jewish student of the scriptures, and it was to the scriptures that Jesus referred the lawyer to answer his own question: Love of God with heart, soul, strength, and mind is demanded throughout the Old Testament. Leviticus (19:18) had specifically added the injunction to love one's neighbor as oneself.

So that was the ready answer, and Jesus acknowledged its correctness. But then came the hard question: "And who is my neighbor?"

What a question for that time and place! The Jews to whom Jesus was trying to bring His gospel prided themselves as God's chosen people and despised those not so chosen. Separated by God through selection and covenant, they had separated themselves by self-righteousness and pride. Well might such a people ask, "Who is my brother?"

How should He answer? He who had cautioned about the

141

folly of casting pearls before swine knew well that His listeners were not ready for a sermon on the universality of the gospel and the brotherhood of man. Yet the teaching moment was here and must not be lost.

With His genius for taking people where they were, talking in terms of their everyday experience, the Master Teacher gave, as He so frequently did, a parable, one of the greatest of His ministry. Of His forty or so recorded parables, none surpasses that of the Good Samaritan for the power of its unmistakable message.

"A certain man went down from Jerusalem to Jericho, and fell among thieves. . . ."

His listeners must have nodded; they knew well that road through the barren Judean hills, only twenty miles long but dropping three thousand feet in elevation as it wound through the narrow canyons. They called it "the bloody way" for the robber bands infesting the limestone caves there.

In simple, unadorned words Jesus told the story; the traveler robbed, wounded, and left for dead, ignored by the priest and the Levite who passed that way, saved at considerable risk and inconvenience by a "certain Samaritan."

Then came the searching question: "Which now of these three, thinkest thou, was neighbour unto him that fell among the thieves?"

And the answer, unarguable even to those prideful people who so despised the Samaritans: "He that shewed mercy on him."

What profundity lies in this simple parable! In those few words, Jesus condemned the narrowness that afflicted Judaism and afflicts so much of the world today. He condemned the discrimination implied in the question, "Who is my neighbor?" He taught service through love, not duty. He turned the question, "Who is my neighbor?" to the far more pointed, meaningful one, "Whose neighbor am I?"

Would you know who is your neighbor? Become a neighbor to all through the service of love. Let there be no more

142

separation of man. That is what Christ's parable taught. That is the heart of the Christian message. How timeless and universal is that message. It speaks—or should—to us whenever we cross the street to avoid the vagrant slumped against the wall, whenever we hurry away from an accident scene rather than get involved as a witness, whenever we despise or shun or fear others because they are not of our race or nationality or political persuasion.

To Latter-day Saints the parable of the Good Samaritan should strike home with particular force. We count ourselves as a "peculiar" people, peculiar in the sense of being chosen, covenanted, warned to be in the world but not of the world, much as God called and separated ancient Israel.

Jesus condemned the folly and evil of separating ourselves in pride and self-righteousness. He taught that where much is given much is required, and that what He most earnestly expects is that we love and serve without discrimination.

To us of all people comes the searching question: "Whose neighbor am I?"

WHOM DO WE SEND AWAY?

It was in one of those Sunday evening "study groups." Half a dozen couples, good friends, comfortable with each other, had been meeting together for years. This night the talk turned to the question of neighborliness; how could the Church change the perception many people have that Mormons tend to be clannish and shut others out?

One man cut to the heart of the question. "How many of us," he asked, "belong to any kind of small, intimate group that includes non-Mormons as well as Mormons?" The silence was uncomfortable as it became clear where the problem lay.

"Now my brethren, we see that God is mindful of every people, whatsoever land they may be in; yea, he numbereth his people, and his bowels of mercy are over all the earth...." (Alma 26:37.)

That testimony of God's concern for all people came with conviction from a man who knew what he was talking about. Ammon and his three brothers, sons of Mosiah, had just risked their lives on a mission among the Lamanites. Even survival among those wild and warlike people was questionable; what hope could they have for conversions?

But God is mindful of all people. He touched Lamanite hearts. So complete was the conversion of thousands of them that they vowed to kill no more, buried their weapons of war, prostrated themselves before their enemies, and "praised God even in the very act of perishing under the sword." Such love of their fellow men had not been seen before; not even, Ammon noted, among his own people, the Nephites.

That challenging observation speaks to us today. Members of Christ's church ought to be second to no one in living the principle He taught so earnestly—that we love our neighbor.

God has given us so much. He only asks that we share our abundance. Alma spoke of such sharing: "And now, because of the steadiness of the church they began to be exceedingly rich, having abundance of all things whatsoever they stood in need—an abundance of flocks and herds, and fatlings of every kind, and also abundance of grain, and of gold, and of silver, and of precious things...." (Alma 1:29.)

We, too, have an abundance of things like that. But "because of the steadiness of the Church" we have abundance of even more precious things. In our wards, we have an abundance of friendship. We have an abundance of sociability. We have an abundance of brotherhood, of caring, of bearing each other's burdens and sharing each other's joys. We have an abundance of neighborliness.

With that abundance, can we follow the example of Alma's people: "And thus, in their prosperous circumstances, they did not send away any who were naked, or that were hungry, or that were athirst, or that were sick, or that had not been nourished ... they were liberal to all, both old and young, both bond and free, both male and female, whether out of the church or in the church, having no respect to persons as to those who stood in need." (Alma 1:30.)

There are among us those who are hungry for neighborliness. There are naked among us: people hit by tragedy or adversity and without the support system of home and visiting teachers, bishops, priesthood quorums and the Relief Society. There are those who thirst, who may be sick, who need the nourishment of love and caring that we as good neighbors can bring.

Happy in the comfortable sufficiency of our ward families and preoccupied with family and Church responsibilities, do we unknowingly or unthinkingly "send away" people like that?

MEASURING OUR HEARTS

In "The Wizard of Oz" is a passage that cries out for understanding and, when understood, tells us much of what we need to do.

The tin man is looking for a heart. In his search, he encounters the wizard, who teaches him the profound truth: "It is not how much you love, my friend, but by how much you are loved, that a heart is measured."

We are taught to love. Loving God and loving our neighbors are the first two commandments. Part of the Savior's mission was to teach us, by example and by precept, to love.

But just loving is not enough. What the Savior taught over and over — and what the wizard was saying — is that love cannot be passive. Unless it leads us to service, unless it causes us to reach out, to live the kind of life, be the kind of person, that is loved by others, it is not really love; at least it is not Christlike love.

So we love our neighbor, including our non-Mormon neighbor. What do we do about it? Do we love him enough that he loves us? There are potential barriers to that kind of relationship. One is the nature of Mormonism. It is so fulfilling. It takes so much of our time and energies. It enriches us with such rewarding relationships and fills our lives in such satisfying ways that it is easy to slip into the rut of treating with benign neglect those who are not also involved.

A more pernicious barrier may grow, if we are not careful, from our conviction of the rightness of our beliefs and life-style. Such conviction can lead to rejection of those with different beliefs and life-styles. Or, in our eagerness to share what we have with others, it can lead into the trap of viewing non-Mormon neighbors and associates only as potential converts, not as friends who can enrich our lives.

That is not what the Savior taught. And it is not what His servants are teaching. We have been repeatedly exhorted by the General Authorities to love our neighbors, and specifically warned that differences in personal standards and social activities cannot justify ostracism of or unkindness toward those of other beliefs.

If the heart is judged by how much one is loved, people who fall into that unkindness trap will be found wanting.

But there's another reason than the fear of judgment for reaching out to others. Diversity can be so enriching. There is so much to learn, so much to enjoy, from the many good people of other cultures and other religions who live among us.

Such a man died recently. And another such man spoke at his funeral. "One does not have to be an especially brilliant student of the likes and dislikes of the Deity to be confident that the Lord loves a cheerful man," the speaker said. "God somehow seems to put on this earth a sufficient number of joyful persons to keep the rest of us from drowning in our own tears.

"The Creator, no matter who or what we perceive Him to be, put us on this earth to get along with one another, to cherish our being together, to love each other in gratitude for His having put us here and in anticipation of our rejoining Him at some unknown but inevitable time.

"Loving all people was the nature of our friend. Each of us knew that instantly when first we met him. The warmth of his greeting told us; the happiness of his smile.

"None of his virtues could remain hidden in the sunshine of his personality.

"He loved his neighbor not because it is mandatory but because he instinctively knew that was the way to live on this earth, and the only way."

All this was truly said; he was just such a man. There are many such men and women among us, and many such men as he who gave the eulogy.

How much poorer are we, how much we deprive ourselves if we fail to make such neighbors our friends.

FOR THE SERVICE OF LOVE

How slow they were to learn, these twelve men who called themselves disciples. For three years they had sat at Jesus' feet, listened to His gospel of love and service, watched as He ministered to the poor, the despised, the leprous.

They had heard Him say, plainly, "Whosoever will be chief among you, let him be your servant." (Matt. 20:27.) He had taught them specifically, when invited to a feast, to take a lower place, for "whosoever exalteth himself shall be abased; and he that humbleth himself shall be exalted." (Luke 14:11.)

Now here they were at the sacred Passover, the last they would share with Him, and they were wrangling over who should be greatest among them. Jesus made no comment. What He did was far more eloquent: "He riseth from supper, and laid aside his garments; and took a towel, and girded himself.

"After that he poureth water into a bason, and began to wash the disciples' feet, and to wipe them with the towel wherewith he was girded." (John 13:4-5.)

This was the role of a slave, the girded towel the badge of slavedom. How more impressively could He have demonstrated the central message of His ministry?

Our finite minds cannot comprehend the agony in Gethsemane when Christ took upon Himself our sins. We can only faintly imagine the agony of flesh pierced by driven nails, of a

150

body hung on a cross to die. The glory and mystery of the Resurrection are far beyond our present understanding.

The washing of the feet, though, we can understand. We recognize it as a profound object lesson in humility and service. We cannot mistake His injunction to follow His example.

That seems clear enough. But do we understand, really? Did the disciples? To Peter he said, "What I do thou knowest not now; but thou shalt know hereafter." (John 13:7.) And to all, after he had finished the ritual and sat down, He asked, "Know ye what I have done to you?" (John 13:12.)

Why such questions? What was there not to understand? Was there something more here than the unmistakable lesson to humble oneself in the service of others?

"If I wash thee not," He warned the protesting Peter, "thou hast no part with me." (John 13:8.)

What Peter did not understand, nor did the others, was that sharing in this ordinance of foot washing meant sharing in the Savior's mission, His service of love to mankind.

But he would learn. Later, on the shore of Galilee, this disciple who three times that awful night had denied his Lord, would hear the Resurrected Christ ask three times, "Simon, son of Jonas, lovest thou me?" Three times he would answer, "Yea Lord, thou knowest I love thee." Three times he would hear the plea: "Feed my sheep," and finally begin to understand what it was Jesus had asked—that we wash and clean our feet for the service of love. (John 21:15-17.)

As they came to that last supper, the disciples had been washed. Earlier they had been baptized. With one exception, they were, Jesus assured them, clean. What He was doing in washing their feet was not forgiving their sins; that had been done. What He was asking was the one thing yet needed—the consecration of their lives to His ministry. As Elder James E. Talmage taught in his book *Jesus the Christ*, "The washing of feet was an ordinance pertaining to the Holy Priesthood, the full import of which they had yet to learn."

That they did learn, finally, through the gift of the Holy

Ghost at Pentecost, is clear from the dedication and courage with which they filled their missions.

Today's apostles carry the same charge, with the same grant of authority. May they have the sustaining prayers of Church members everywhere in their awesome responsibilities.

DARE TO EXCEL

In a peaceful Dearborn, Michigan, suburb stands the palatial home of Henry Ford, now a museum of his life and times. Wandering through it some years ago a visitor opened a desk drawer and discovered an envelope, on the back of which, in Mrs. Ford's handwriting, were the words:

> Bite off more than you can chew, and chew it,
> Dare to do more than you can do, and do it.
> Hitch your wagon to a star,
> Keep your seat,
> And there you are.

Those lines summarize about as well as any the philosophy on which Henry Ford became one of the world's great industrialists, a man whose mass production of an inexpensive car changed American lives forever.

They also reflect the spirit on which was based an organization that was founded and grew to maturity during the same years Henry Ford was building his industrial empire — the Boy Scouts of America.

The Boy Scouts of America was established February 8, 1910. As The Church of Jesus Christ of Latter-day Saints observes February as Scout Month three-quarters of a century later, 300,000 Mormon boys are enrolled in Scouting — 122,000 as

Cub Scouts, 114,000 as Boy Scouts, 37,000 as Varsity Scouts, and 27,000 as Explorers.

Much has changed in Scouting as the organization has tried to keep pace with a changing society. But the fundamentals remain.

"On my honor" ... duty to God and country ... helping other people ... keeping physically strong, mentally awake, morally straight. These are principles that have been central to Scouting from its beginning. They are central today, and — with family breakup and moral breakdown endemic in our society — never have they been more important.

Equally important is the concept on which Scouting thrives: That boys become men — real men — by daring to bite off more than they can chew, and then chewing it. Making that concept a reality takes leaders with the same kind of daring.

It's boldness is almost beyond belief, when you think about it, to imagine a leader can take a group of squirming, chattering eight- to eleven-year-olds and focus their energies and attention through the disciplines of the Cub Scout program. Or give Boy Scout-age youngsters the desire, perseverance, and leadership needed to complete the long, challenging path to Eagle. Or keep mid-teenage boys out of beer halls and the back seats of cars and united in the wholesome, challenging programs of Varsity and Explorer Scouting.

There are so many distractions, so many forces pulling youngsters off in directions that lead anywhere but where they ought to go. How can a leader succeed against such competition?

The wonder is that so many do. Like Ralph Degn of River Heights 34th Ward, Providence Utah Stake. With his calling as Varsity Scout team coach came twenty boys ages thirteen to seventeen whose Church attendance ranged from regular to nonexistent but who were pretty well agreed they wanted nothing more to do with Scouting. Also with the call came a challenge from the stake president: Eagle badges for at least ten of those boys.

He wrestled with that problem and prayed about it, Degn recalled, and an idea came. He cleared it with the bishopric and stake presidency, then met with the group and made them a proposition: a high-level program of activities and trips for those who met the standards.

The requirements were stiff: fill all Eagle requirements, attend seventy-five percent of Church meetings, enroll in seminary each quarter, give two talks in sacrament meeting, earn all money needed for the program.

Eighteen of the twenty made it. River Heights is a different place now. The Eagle service projects included painting all the town's fire hydrants, painting the bleachers and pavilion at the ball park, refurbishing the welcome sign at the edge of town.

"Scouting has become the thing to do in our community, where two years ago it wasn't," one official reported. "Some of these boys were in trouble in the community two years ago; now they have a real sense of community pride."

And from one of the Scouts: "Before the goal was set, no one wanted anything to do with Scouting. Now the whole group has become good friends and they feel they have accomplished something impossible by setting and achieving a long-range goal."

"Bite off more than you can chew. . . . "

RICH TOWARD GOD

It was the beginning of ward conference. To set a tone of brotherhood and spirituality, the week began with a dinner, followed by a temple session.

After the session, the high priest group leader approached the bishop, expressing gratitude for the experience of enjoying the temple in the company of some seventy fellow ward members. Then, lowering his voice and thinking no one else could hear, he added: "And, bishop, don't worry about the ward budget. If this stretches it, I'd like to take care of it."

A small incident, but in character. This man, a lawyer, had performed countless acts of quiet generosity, giving his means, his time, and his professional skills to those in need. He knew well, and practiced, the principle of stewardship.

How earnestly and persistently the Savior tried to teach that principle. It is estimated that nearly half of His teachings relate to the proper use of wealth.

There was the time (see Luke 12), for example, when Jesus was speaking to a multitude so dense they stepped on each other's toes. He spoke of the love and concern of the Father for every human being. He taught them to be guided by the Holy Ghost.

As though he had heard not a word of that divine message, a young man spoke up: "Master, speak to my brother that he divide the inheritance with me."

The Savior must have grieved over the thoughtlessness of that rude interruption. But He gave no sign. With His genius for seizing the teaching moment, He abruptly changed His discourse: "Take heed, and beware of covetousness: for a man's life consisteth not in the abundance of things which he possesseth." (Luke 12:15.)

The parable of the rich fool followed. It has been called an American parable, and with good reason; it condemns directly the covetousness reflected in the bumper sticker seen on American luxury cars: "He who gets the most toys wins." Well might it also be called the retirement parable.

Jesus spoke of the rich man whose lands bore so abundantly he had no room to store his crops. "And he said, This will I do: I will pull down my barns, and build greater; and there will I bestow all my fruits and my goods.

"And I will say to my soul, Soul, thou hast much goods laid up for many years; take thine ease, eat, drink, and be merry.

"But God said unto him, Thou fool, this night thy soul shall be required of thee: then whose shall these things be, which thou hast provided?" (Luke 12:18-20.)

Why such harsh condemnation? Was this not a provident man who had worked hard all his life, saved his money and invested wisely, and now deserved to retire in comfort? Isn't that the American ideal? Where had he failed?

He had failed to recognize the principle of stewardship. In his eyes, they were *his* barns, *his* fruits, *his* goods. He had forgotten, if he ever knew, that the earth is the Lord's and the fullness thereof, that every material thing we possess is by His sufferance and only temporarily.

Having forgotten that, it was only natural that his use of his wealth was so self-centered. All of it was to go into his enlarged barn for his ease. There was no thought of sharing, no concern for the poor, no awareness of brotherhood.

No wonder that He whose entire ministry was centered around sharing and brotherhood should condemn such self-

157

ishness and then, to all of us, warn: "So is he that layeth up treasure for himself, and is not rich toward God." (Luke 12:21.)

There is a stewardship, too, of time and energy and talents—all of them also gifts from God. He condemns selfish use of them as well, particularly their use to take our ease.

The Savior's attitude toward retirement from service to God and mankind is unmistakable. "Woe to them that are at ease in Zion," he warns. (Amos 6:1; 2 Ne. 28:24.) His appeals to endure to the end are almost beyond counting.

Instead of building bigger barns, what if the rich man gave his surplus wealth to charity? What if he endowed a missionary fund? What if instead of taking his ease, he and his wife accepted a mission call? What if they became temple workers or name extractors or dedicated themselves to any of the countless other opportunities for doing good?

The happiness reflected in the faces of those so engaged, by contrast with those who try to fill their retirement with recreation and self-gratifying pursuits, is obvious here and now. Hereafter what a difference there must be between those who lay up treasure for themselves and those who are rich toward God.

INQUIRING FOR OURSELVES

Illustrating his priesthood lesson, the teacher recalled the day, many years ago, when his father came home from quorum meeting, chuckling and wiping moist eyes.

"Father had taught the High Priests for thirty-five years. On this day he said to me, 'Son, don't ever underestimate the strength of the gospel.' And then he told what had happened that day."

He was in the middle of the lesson, he said, when an elderly man raised his hand. He was a humble man, a man of the soil, who usually sat quietly listening. On this day his voice rang with conviction: "I have studied this lesson. I have thought a great deal about it. I have read everything I can find in the scriptures on the subject. I've prayed about it.

"And, brethren, I have decided the Lord was right."

In some cultures, in some churches, that would sound like blasphemy. What arrogance that such a man should presume to decide whether or not the Lord was right.

But the teacher — and his father — saw it differently: "What power, what majesty, there is in a church that expects its people to decide for themselves."

What majesty, yes. And what responsibility.

Joseph Smith spoke of that responsibility: "All men have the privilege of thinking for themselves upon all matters related to conscience. . . . We are not disposed . . . to deprive anyone of exercising that free independence of mind which heaven has bestowed upon the human family as one of its choicest gifts."

So did Brigham Young: "I am more afraid that this people have so much confidence in their leaders that they will not inquire for themselves of God whether they are led by Him. I am fearful that they settle down in a state of blind self-security, trusting their eternal destiny in the hands of their leaders with a reckless confidence that in itself would thwart the purposes of God in their salvation. . . . Let every man and woman know, by the whispering of the Spirit of God to themselves, whether their leaders are walking in the path the Lord dictates, or not. . . ." (*Journal of Discourses* 9:150.)

Where there is such privilege, such responsibility, there is also risk. The risk is that independence of thought and inquiry can become reliance on one's own knowledge, one's own wisdom.

The Lord's judgment is heavy on those who "put down the power and miracles of God, and preach up unto themselves their own wisdom and their own learning." (2 Ne. 26:20.) "Wo be unto him that hearkeneth unto the precepts of men, and denieth the power of God, and the gift of the Holy Ghost! Yea, wo be unto him that saith: We have received, and we need no more!" (2 Ne. 28:25-26.)

So how do we avoid that trap? How can we safely know the line between the independent inquiry the Lord urges upon us and the prideful self-reliance He condemns?

That humble farmer in the priesthood quorum knew the line. He knew that the confirmation he was seeking did not lie within his own powers, but in study of the word of God and in asking God directly for an answer.

The Lord has promised us, speaking of His servants, that "Whatsoever they shall speak when moved upon by the Holy Ghost shall be scripture, shall be the will of the Lord, shall be the mind of the Lord, shall be the word of the Lord, shall be the voice of the Lord, and the power of God unto salvation." (D&C 68:4.)

That is clear and powerful and assuring. But it raises a question: How can we know for ourselves when they are moved upon by the Holy Ghost?

Brigham Young said: "Were your faith concentrated upon the proper object, your confidence unshaken, your lives pure and holy, every one fulfilling the duties of his or her calling according to the Priesthood and capacity bestowed upon you, you would be filled with the Holy Ghost, and it would be impossible for any man to deceive you." (*Journal of Discourses* 7:227.)

That is the power and majesty—and responsibility—bestowed upon us by the gospel of Jesus Christ.

WHICH WAY THE SHORE?

Some years ago, the news wires carried from Falls River, Massachusetts, the account of a river tragedy.

A group of girls sunning themselves on the bank heard a call: "Which way the shore?" They looked, saw a young man swimming in the river, and chuckled at his way of fooling around. Again came the call: "Which way the shore?" They looked and wondered, briefly, then went back to their suntan lotion and girl talk. Again, urgently: "Which way the shore?" Recognizing, at last, the desperation in his voice, they called to him, and one went for help.

It was too late. While they watched, the boy sank and drowned. When his body was recovered, they found he was blind.

Those girls didn't deliberately abandon him to die. They would have saved him had they realized he was in trouble, had they been really listening, had their self-absorption not deafened the inner ear.

How many of us are like them, so absorbed in the minutiae of daily living, so self-oriented we cannot hear with the inner ear? And how many of our fellow men are like him? How many are silently calling for help?

"Neglect not the gift that is in thee, . . . given thee by prophecy, with the laying on of the hands of the presbytery," Paul exhorted us. (1 Tim. 4:14.) One of those gifts of the Spirit is that of discernment. At no time is it more nobly exercised than in hearing—and heeding—the unspoken cry of one in need.

The Savior, as always, set the perfect example: ". . . as he went the people thronged him. And a woman having an issue of blood twelve years, which had spent all her living upon physicians, neither could be healed of any, came behind him, and touched the border of his garment: and immediately her issue of blood stanched.

"And Jesus said, Who touched me? When all denied, Peter and they that were with him said, Master, the multitude throng thee and press thee, and sayest thou, Who touched me?" (Luke 8:42-45.)

The multitude throng and press us as well. The world with all its challenges and distractions is very much with us. While we cannot respond to a touch with the immediacy and finality of the Savior, we can, if we listen with the heart, discern in the cacophony of daily living the silent call for help.

We all know people who exercise that special gift, and whom the Savior must love in a special way. There is a sister down the block with a handicapped child of her own who always seems to be there to help carry the handicaps of others. It is she who sees in the face of a young mother struggling with three or four preschool children the need for a few hours of relief and takes over. It is she who senses in a slumped shoulder or a dejected posture that something is wrong at home, and is there the next day with warm bread and warm words, ready to weep together or laugh together or kneel in prayer together as the listening heart decrees.

There is the business executive, the shop foreman, the high school teacher whose listening heart hears the call, "Which way the shore?" and sets aside the daily routine to take up the infinitely more important task of ministering to a human soul.

There are those who have what we call the "missionary spirit," which is nothing more than the listening heart ever alert to the silent cry of one seeking the safety of a spiritual shore. The cry can come at any time, from the new neighbor, the airliner seatmate, the lady at the checkout counter, the classmate at school. The listening heart, sensing spiritual need, responds: "This way. Here is safety. Here is the gospel of Jesus Christ."

Upon those safely on the shore lies a sacred responsibility. Alma described it, speaking of those who: " . . . are desirous to come into the fold of God, and to be called his people, and are willing to bear one another's burdens, that they may be light; Yea, and are willing to mourn with those that mourn; yea, and comfort those that stand in need of comfort, and to stand as witnesses of God at all times and in all things, and in all places. . . ." (Mosiah 18:8-9.)

Such as these are qualified to listen, to hear, and to confidently cry, "Here is the shore!"

INDEX